C   t
for a
Perfect
Wedding

SIXTH EDITION

Check List for a Perfect Wedding

SIXTH EDITION

BARBARA LEE FOLLETT
LOULIE HYDE SUTRO

BROADWAY BOOKS
New York

Book design by Gretchen Achilles

Library of Congress Cataloging-in-Publication Data

Follett, Barbara Lee.
Check list for a perfect wedding / Barbara Lee Follett,
Loulie Hyde Sutro.—6th ed.
p. cm.
Rev. ed. of: Check list for a perfect wedding.
Garden City, N.Y.: Doubleday, 1986.
Includes index.
1. Wedding etiquette. I. Sutro, Loulie Hyde. II. Title.
BJ2051 .F6 2002
395.2'2—dc21   2002023231

ISBN 0-7679-1233-0

3   5   7   9   10   8   6   4

Contents

First Thoughts

You are engaged. Best wishes to you and your fiancé for all the happiness in the world—now and for always!

Now that the exciting and sometimes hectic fun of planning your wedding is before you, *Check List* is here to help with every aspect of this thrilling and often overwhelming endeavor.

If your engagement has not already been announced, please refer to page 17 for a full guide to various ways to make that announcement, notify newspapers and attend to other preliminaries. If these activities have been taken care of, then on to the main event—your wedding.

Wedding plans equal lists, and lists equal efficiency. This checklist has been compiled just for you, giving you the perfect formula for your perfect wedding—correct, complete and in chronological order. Just follow the items of instruction one by one as they are listed, referring to the appropriate chapters in the book for information. When you have taken care of each item, check it off. If an item does not fit your plan, *cross it off and forget it.* When you have considered and attended to all the items, you will have achieved your perfect wedding with a minimum of confusion.

While this checklist is addressed to happy brides-to-be the world over, it is designed equally for the grooms, the mothers and any involved family members and friends. You will see where some sections seem to be directed to the bride and others to the mother. These are for the most part interchangeable; the most important aspect is to get the item completed and checked off when it needs to be!

My own role was that of mother of the bride, and I found that while the bride blissfully floated along on her personal cloud, many of the more earthly tasks fell to me. We have all attended many weddings, but we tend to overlook the details. This is as it *should* be. The machinery behind a carefully planned wedding is never evident, but it is always there.

How many mothers of a bride-to-be have awakened in the middle of the night startled by unanswered questions?

"How do I cope with Ted's mother *and* his stepmother?"

"What number can I give the caterer when so many guests still haven't responded?"

"What is Sue supposed to do with seven salad bowls?"

Having found the answers to these and every other question that needed answering, I noted them. I saved my checklist at the request of many friends who sensed that the serenity and beauty of our daughter's wedding could have been achieved only through meticulous planning. From my notes, followed by deep personal research, came the original edition of *Check List for a Perfect Wedding*.

It is my good fortune—and yours, too, I hope—that Doubleday approved the periodic revisions and updatings that have taken place over the years. Continual research, questions from friends and strangers, and my question-and-answer columns have kept me in touch with a variety of problems and situations from diverse sources. Now on the way to two million copies, we celebrate with yet another newly revised, updated and expanded edition.

Brides and their mothers will know that by the wedding day it is too late to change plans, remedy mistakes or add forgotten details. Rely on this new book with confidence, and know that *all* will be done, and done *well*.

There are those rare people who thrive under last-minute pressure. They have the physical and emotional makeup that lets them work under that kind of tension, and miraculously, some get by. If you are like that, *Bravo!* and I hope your luck continues. Most of us learn to expect the unexpected, however, and that we must provide time for it. This leeway time is essential in planning a wedding and reception, when so many separate, isolated details must meld at zero hour—the wedding day.

How often do I hear, "Can you believe it? I've called four of the best photographers, and they've been booked for months!" Another wail comes from a bride-to-be who just discovered she was too late for delivery of the gown she "adored." Nine months to a year or more is none too soon to begin *all* your arrangements.

The traditional wedding in all its glory is more popular than ever. Make your plans, but always remember your objective—a happy, serene, memorable day, not a stage production.

Magazine and newspaper articles headline the high cost of weddings. Yes, they can be, and often are, but this is up to you. Feel confident that the elaborateness and cost of your wedding will not make it outstanding, so do not put a financial strain on your parents or yourself and your groom. With much thought and careful planning item by item, you can arrange your flawless wedding while staying within your means. You will find throughout *Check List* numerous ideas for prudently keeping expenses down; frequently the book will suggest workable alternatives. *Never economize on effort and planning*, however—they are the essential factors that will make your wedding beautiful!

In our diverse society, marriages sometimes bring together persons of different cultures. Each has something of value to contribute, providing the opportunity to incorporate customs or traditions from each culture. To do so is not a compromise but, rather, a meaningful addition to your ceremony, and to your lives together.

Toward the end of this book you will find chapters on second marriages, home/garden weddings and nontraditional weddings. These chapters were written so that *Check List* will be helpful to any bride in any wedding situation.

Since the original version of *Check List for a Perfect Wedding* was written, computers have become an integral part of almost all of our lives. Computers can be invaluable, with a variety of websites and software programs to help you with everything from guest lists and table seating to budgeting, gift registry and catering suggestions. All of these are available for referral, while you rely on the basic and trustworthy information found in this compact and portable *Check List*, your primary resource for wedding planning. Although there is no question that a lovely wedding can be planned *without* the use of a computer, our website, www.weddingschecklist.com, is available to complement your use of *Check List for a Perfect Wedding*.

Weddings *should* be fun, and yours *will* be if your nerves are not frayed by too many details. Go to sleep each night with the assurance that when you awaken the next day, you have only to consult your *Check List*. It will do the worrying for you. Relax. Enjoy the excitement and have fun.

Barbara Lee Follett
(MRS. BENJAMIN N. FOLLETT III)

With updates and revisions by *Loulie Hyde Sutro*
(MRS. JOHN A. SUTRO, JR.)

The Master Checklist

The following checklist is your secret to a perfect wedding. Keep this book handy—even carry it with you.

• I want you to feel comfortable that everything you will need is contained here. Consider spending time browsing through the entire book to give you a sense that you are in good hands and "all will be revealed."

You will often use the sections titled "Important Contacts" and "Notes" as convenient places to record special names, addresses and telephone numbers.

The Checklist items in bold type are discussed in depth; just refer to the section of the book in which they are included, or look up key words in the index. Items not bolded speak for themselves.

ANNOUNCING YOUR ENGAGEMENT

(See pages 17 to 26.)

☐ **Tell your parents and your fiancé's parents.**

☐ **Arrange for your families to meet.**

☐ Announce to your friends.

☐ Contact your local newspapers.

GETTING STARTED

(See pages 28 to 41.)

☐ Decide what type of wedding you will have, the degree of formality and the approximate size.

☐ Engage a bridal consultant, if you wish.

☐ Set the date and hour for the wedding.

☐ Reserve the venue for the wedding and rehearsal, and make certain the officiator is available.

☐ If it is to be a church wedding, arrange a time for you and your fiancé to talk with the clergyman.

☐ Plan church arrangements.

☐ Reserve the reception venue, one that is large enough to hold a 75 percent rate of acceptance.

GETTING YOUR TEAM IN PLACE

(See pages 42 to 60.)

☐ Engage the caterer and make preliminary plans.

☐ Engage the florist and set a date for a conference.

☐ Engage the photographer and a video camera person, if you plan to have one or both.

☐ Arrange for music at the wedding.

☐ Engage musicians for the reception.

ARRANGING THE WEDDING PARTY

(See pages 61 to 80.)

☐ Select the bridesmaids, maid or matron of honor, ushers, best man and others.

☐ Ensure the groom is aware of his responsibilities.

☐ Confer with the groom's family concerning their participation and responsibilities.

A LITTLE PAPERWORK

(See pages 81 to 94.)

☐ Copy all wedding party names, addresses, phone numbers, faxes and e-mail addresses into the back of this book and into your computer or card file.

☐ With input from both families as well as the bride and groom, begin to put together a guest list in your computer or card file; set a deadline for final lists.

☐ Make a detailed calendar for the months preceding your wedding date.

☐ Purchase a notebook in which to record wedding gifts as they arrive.

☐ Plan activities for out-of-town attendees.

☐ Announce your engagement in the press.

☐ Prepare your home for house guests.

GETTING INTO IT

(See pages 95 to 130.)

☐ If the reception is to be at a home, begin planning logistics, décor and any necessary refurbishing.

☐ Select and purchase (or order) your wedding gown and veil.

☐ Select and purchase wedding shoes and break them in.

☐ Select and arrange for attendants' dresses and head-pieces; advise them about shoes, jewelry, makeup and accessories.

☐ Advise the mothers on dress colors so they may make their selections.

☐ Decide on the men's attire.

☐ Whether hiring limousines or using friends, contract (or arrange) all wedding party transportation to the ceremony and from the ceremony to the reception.

☐ Order stationery.

☐ Select and register for silver, china, crystal and housewares; list the stores in the back of this book, as well as in your computer or card file.

☐ Readvise all family members of the invitation list deadline.

☐ Select and purchase your going-away outfit and trousseau.

☐ Plan for your married living arrangements.

☐ Follow up with bridesmaids and ushers in terms of what they will wear and the fittings that will be involved.

☐ Make appointments for medical and dental check-ups; have a blood test if required.

☐ Order wedding invitations and announcements.

☐ Calendar a date to mail invitations six to eight weeks before the wedding.

☐ Decide upon the particulars of your wedding reception.

GIFTS AND APPOINTMENTS

(See pages 131 to 144.)

☐ Promptly open and catalog all wedding gifts as they come in, and plan for them.

☐ Keep up with your thank-you notes.

- ☐ Check your calendar and pace the timing of your appointments, parties and engagements.

- ☐ Arrange for bridal gown fittings as necessary.

- ☐ Prepare guest lists for those who have offered to entertain for you.

- ☐ Schedule bridal showers and parties with your friends.

- ☐ Coordinate other parties.

- ☐ Send a schedule of shower and party dates to the bridal party.

- ☐ Remind the groom to get a blood test if required.

- ☐ Select the groom's ring if it is to be a double-ring ceremony, and have it engraved.

- ☐ Select a wedding gift for the groom (optional).

- ☐ Select keepsake-type gifts for the bridesmaids, flower girl and ring bearer.

- ☐ Remind the groom to select gifts for his ushers.

- ☐ Order thank-you (hostess) gifts or flowers for those who entertain for you.

- ☐ Remind the groom to reserve rental suits for the male members of the bridal party.

- ☐ Check your luggage and plan your packing for the honeymoon.

☐ If you choose, plan a family champagne/wine tasting party to make appropriate selections.

☐ Change your name on all important business papers (insurance, credit cards, bank accounts, legal documents, driver's license), if applicable.

☐ See your attorney about making a will.

☐ Make an appointment for hair, manicure, pedicure and trial makeup early in the week before the wedding.

☐ Schedule hair and makeup appointments for yourself and your bridesmaids the day of the wedding.

IT'S GETTING CLOSE NOW!

(See pages 145 to 165.)

☐ Address and stamp wedding invitations and announcements.

☐ Research where you want your wedding publicized and the publication policy of each newspaper. *(See pages 26, 87 to 89.)*

☐ Plan housing arrangements for the out-of-town bridal attendants. *(See pages 89 to 91.)*

☐ Arrange for valet parking, shuttles and/or an off-duty policeman to direct traffic and provide security, if necessary.

☐ Keep the groom's family up to date on the guest list and wedding gifts received.

☐ **Arrange a place for the bride and bridesmaids to dress on the wedding day.**

☐ **Arrange a venue for wedding photographs.** *(See pages 55 to 56.)*

☐ If you are a member of the officiating clergyman's church, or if you know him, arrange for your mother to hand-deliver a wedding invitation to him and his wife.

☐ Calendar a time to go with the groom to get a marriage license.

☐ **Arrange a bachelorette party for your bridesmaids.**

☐ Save some ribbons from gift and shower packages for your bridesmaids to make into mock bouquets to use at the wedding rehearsal.

☐ **Arrange for a rehearsal dinner party to be given the night of the rehearsal.**

☐ **Send reserved-pew cards to special guests and family members, or tell them to identify themselves to the ushers so they can be seated in front pews.**

☐ **Select a responsible person to handle the guest book at the reception.**

☐ **Design your wedding program and have it printed.**

☐ **Plan for something old, something new, something borrowed and something blue!**

☐ Recheck all purveyors by phone, including caterer, florist, photographer, video person, musicians, stationer, drivers and parking attendants, wedding dress delivery, church arrangements, cake delivery.

THE HOME STRETCH

(See pages 166 to 175.)

☐ Deliver "weekend packets" to hotels where out-of-town guests will stay.

☐ Think about the wedding rehearsal and make your decisions as early as possible.

☐ Count acceptances for the reception and estimate the number of late responses; notify the caterer.

☐ If you are using them, be sure someone has alphabetized and properly arranged your seating cards at the reception.

☐ Gather in one place everything you will need to dress for the wedding; remind the groom to do the same.

☐ Remind the groom to arrange for the best man to drive the getaway car and check it for gas, or to order a car or taxi.

☐ Remind the maid of honor that it is her duty to inform the bride's parents and the groom's parents when the bride and groom are ready to leave after the reception.

☐ Make sure the head usher understands about the reserved pews and passes the information along to the other ushers.

☐ Plan separate rooms for the bride and groom to change into their "going-away" clothes.

☐ **Pack suitcases for the honeymoon and assemble your going-away outfit.**

☐ You and your parents should read and reread the guest list to familiarize yourselves with the names.

☐ With a hug and a kiss, remind your long-suffering dad to get his clothes ready for the big day.

☐ Turn off the lawn sprinklers, if applicable.

☐ Make sure all cars are filled with gasoline.

☐ Arrange for a supply of sandwiches or snacks for the wedding party, photographers and others who will be assembled prior to the ceremony.

☐ **Plan plenty of time to "dress," with your bridesmaids, if you choose.** *(See pages 153 to 155.)*

☐ Ask a bridesmaid to make up a little emergency kit—safety pins, needle and thread, facial tissue, toiletries—to take to the church.

☐ Make a time chart for the wedding day and tape it to your mirror!

☐ Board all pets on the day of the wedding.

☐ And . . . finally, refer to "After the Wedding." *(See pages 176 to 177.)*

When you have taken care of all the items on this checklist, there is nothing further to concern you. Forget the mechanics and make this a perfect day. Enjoy and savor every moment for the years to come.

Happy wedding!

Announcing Your Engagement

If you have not already announced your engagement, read on. Even if your engagement has been announced, use this section on parties after you settle into your new apartment or home. It will help when you entertain friends who entertained for you, and give you the opportunity to show some of your wedding gifts in use. Later in your married life you will have many occasions to give simple or elaborate parties and will find this chapter handy.

WAYS TO ANNOUNCE

Family First

As soon as you become engaged, your parents and your fiancé's parents must be the very first to know—before you breathe even a word to your best friend. If it is at all possible, tell both sets of parents in person.

If either of you plans to continue your education, you cannot blithely assume that your parents will be enchanted with the idea of subsidizing you. You had better find out how they feel about it. The size and cost of your wedding might depend upon the outcome of a frank talk about finances. Your parents might give you a choice between a lavish wedding or the money they would have spent on it.

It is customary for the groom's family to take the next step, which is to arrange a meeting with the your parents. The objective of such a meeting is to create a friendly and harmonious relationship. If, for some reason, the groom's parents do not take the first step in arranging a get-together, the bride's parents can graciously take the initiative.

Announcing to Friends

Take your choice:

- *Simply call your best friends* and let them spread the news. They will!

- A *small family dinner*. Your father or other relative will announce the engagement by proposing a toast to you and your fiancé.

- A *cocktail party* or *cocktail buffet*.

- A *tea* (old-fashioned, but always appropriate).

A Cocktail Party or Cocktail Buffet

A cocktail party is a delightful way to announce your engagement, especially to introduce an out-of-town fiancé to friends.

Although everyone has attended cocktail parties, it is amazing how many questions you must answer, and decisions you must make, when you are about to give your own first party.

You may want to attempt to surprise the guests, so think of an attractive way to divulge the news. Napkins and matchbook covers (with the decline in smoking these are now made with notepads inside) imprinted with the engaged couple's names are somewhat standard. Photographs or clever mantel or door decorations can tell the surprise. Use your ingenuity or originality. Your father or another relative can announce the news by proposing a toast to you and your fiancé.

How many should be invited? Decide how many guests you can accommodate comfortably without wall-to-wall people and intolerably high decibel levels. Depending on the season of the year, perhaps you have a usable garden or deck to handle an overflow. A general rule of thumb is that 75 percent of those invited will attend.

How long should it last? A two-hour period is average, somewhat longer for a cocktail buffet. Guests seldom arrive at the earliest time, so count on a midperiod crunch.

Should there be a receiving line? In recent years,

there seems to have developed a great receiving line debate. Many of the younger generation, and some of the older, feel it is tiresome to stand in line all that time at the beginning of a celebration. There are others, however, who welcome the opportunity to meet and greet everyone at once and then go on to enjoy the party. The choice is up to you.

If yours is to be a large party and you decide to have a receiving line, plan carefully. A receiving line can get bogged down despite the best intentions, and it is a pity for anyone to spend a long time waiting in line instead of mixing at the party. Position the receiving line far enough into the room so that the guests will not feel "stuck" outside—perhaps literally outside the building. Be sure to notify all members of the receiving line to keep discussions with guests brief. You may also plan a receiving line for a certain amount of time, then disband it and circulate.

Unless circumstances make it impossible for the groom's parents to attend the party, they should be part of the receiving line. The receiving line order of positions should be: mother of the bride, father of the bride, mother of the groom, father of the groom, bride-to-be, her groom-to-be.

To speed things up, the parents may spell each other in the receiving line. In a receiving line it is easy to blank out and forget a name—even one's best friend—so don't worry if it happens. An advance review of the guest list usually helps, but fortunately a considerate guest will quickly give his or her name to jog your memory. You may also ask a friend or family member to assist—to greet, introduce and direct guests toward the line.

Should your party be just cocktails or a cocktail buffet? Substantial food or merely "nibbles"? At a cocktail party or open house, hors d'oeuvres alone are sufficient, and guests expect no more. You can serve made-ahead cold canapés or elaborate hot and cold varieties, and you may opt to do it yourself or have help.

At a cocktail buffet, there are various ways to extend the menu, if you are so inclined, without becoming involved in a total buffet dinner. The idea is to give your guests enough to eat so that they will not feel the need to go out for dinner afterward. Never invite some to stay for the buffet and not others—VIP treatment for all or none.

What about invitations? Only after you complete your plan and are ready to be definitive can you send the invitations. Written or printed invitations are time-savers for large parties, while inviting by telephone is more personal for small parties. Instant refusals will give you time to substitute other people. An invitation by e-mail is time-saving, indeed, but less gracious. Never use a fax. You may follow telephoned invitations with mailed reminder cards a week or ten days in advance, although reminders are used more often for dinners than for cocktails.

The reminder card is similar to the invitation diagrammed below. At the top of the card write the words "To remind" and delete the RSVP and phone number. (You may use this same form when you host a party to honor a friend. Just insert the words "To honor

Mr. and Mrs. James Perry Standish

Cocktails
Friday, June 4ᵀᴴ
6:00-8:30

RSVP

75 Evergreen Drive
Danville, Kansas

[Sandra Smith]" either above or below the engraved names.)

Fill-in and printed cards from a stationer come in almost unlimited variety. Although there is usually no time delay for fill-in cards, be sure to plan an extra week or two for printing. The slightly more formal engraved calling cards or French notes are convenient to use, especially if they already include the address.

RSVP is also correct, even preferable. "Regrets only" usually indicates a large party. I prefer responses as insurance against invitations going astray—which they do with increasing frequency!

Seldom does one issue formal third-person (i.e., "*Mr. and Mrs. John Smith* are pleased to invite . . .") invitations for cocktails, except for a formal reception.

What about serving drinks? If you have to choose between having a bartender *or* kitchen help, choose the bartender—professional or moonlighter. Kitchen work can be done ahead of time, whereas tending bar could consume a host's entire evening.

If you plan to have a full open bar as well as beer, water, soft drinks, wine and/or champagne, provide the bartender with a jigger, and tell him exactly what strength drinks you wish him to pour. Nothing can sabotage a party faster than a bartender with a heavy hand. To serve superstrong drinks is unkind to unsuspecting guests—even dangerous. If you plan to have underage guests, notify the bartender not to serve them alcohol. Professional bartenders understand this law.

In terms of quantities, 1 liter serves 22 drinks @ 1½ ounces (7 to 8 persons); 1 bottle of wine serves 5 drinks @ 5 ounces (wineglasses should be only partially filled); 1 gallon of wine serves 26 drinks @ 5 ounces. To be safe, figure 3 drinks per person and have an abundance of extra glasses, as guests tend to put their glasses down, forget where and then order a fresh drink.

Oversupply rather than run short. Nothing need be wasted. At the time you place your order, discuss returns with the store manager. Most bottle shops will credit or exchange the unopened surplus. If you bought at a discount price, however, you may have to keep the extra for future use.

Set up several bar stations to keep people from overcrowding one area. Waiters may also circulate among guests to take orders. At very informal gatherings the host may offer "courtesy of the bar" (guests may help themselves), but his responsibility does not end there. He needs to check the bar often to replenish ice, sodas and other supplies, and he should encourage guests to replenish their own drinks.

Start now to keep detailed records every time you entertain—even for one or two people. You might wonder what value these records have, but you will find that a hostess book will serve you well time and time again—almost like having an extra brain! Record the guests' names, menu, table arrangements, flowers and shopping lists. The following day, add your personal comments about what would make the next time easier or better. Hospitality and easy entertaining, aided by your records, will make your friends' lives and your own more pleasant.

Engagement Teas

Although a cocktail party is often preferred for an engagement announcement, many brides still delight in the charm and tradition of the gracious and old-fashioned engagement tea. The popularity of formal teas waxes and wanes, but never seems to disappear entirely.

The decorations at an engagement tea can be more sentimental and frilly than at other teas, and you will want to think of an attractive way to divulge the news. Some of the same ideas as for a cocktail party can be used, such as imprinted napkins, photographs and door decorations. Use your creativity!

For a large engagement tea, the invitations might state a time to cover a two- or three-hour period, for example from three or four until six o'clock. There is usually a receiving line with the bride-to-be standing between her mother and future mother-in-law. The hostess honors several close friends and relatives by inviting them to pour for half- or three-quarter-hour periods. (At a small tea, one invites friends to come at a specified time, and the hostess pours.) Service for pouring tea and coffee is set up at one or both ends of a dining table. Candles may be lit after five o'clock, or earlier if the day is a dark one. Food can include bite-size tea sandwiches, cookies, candies, nuts and fruit such as stemmed strawberries dipped in chocolate or served next to bowls of powdered and/or brown sugar and sour cream for dipping. If it is summertime, punch or iced tea is a welcome addition. Be sure that food platters are constantly replenished, as guests will come and go during the party. Plan on six to eight sandwiches per person (caterers may say fewer), in four to six varieties. Keep the tea and coffee hot, and be sure the used china is taken to the kitchen immediately.

A Morning Coffee

Everything that applies to the format of a tea also fits the plan of a less-formal morning coffee party, except the hours and the menu. You will still decorate the house with flower arrangements, and have a receiving line or not, as you wish.

Set the hours from ten until twelve o'clock, or nine-thirty until eleven-thirty.

Think of original ways to incorporate morning-type food into your menu: small ham sandwiches, deviled eggs, sausages or chicken livers in a chafing dish, coffee cake, blueberry muffins, English muffins, doughnut "holes," sliced mini-bagels with an assortment of flavored creamed cheese, melon slices, strawberries.

I hope all the preceding information on giving parties and teas will serve you in good stead throughout your married life.

Contact Your Local Newspapers

If you wish, you may have a photograph taken of you and your fiancé for your local newspapers. Contact your papers as to how they prefer to announce engagements, if they do so. They may send you a form to complete. *(See page 87.)*

BREAKING AN ENGAGEMENT

Rarely, but occasionally, it happens. The "it" refers to breaking an engagement or postponing the wedding indefinitely. If you are contemplating such an action, take time to discuss your problems, and do not confuse premarital jitters with a serious basic problem. If, after unemotional consideration, the wedding is canceled, you must take care of a few chores.

If you have already mailed the wedding invitations, you may send a printed card stating that, by mutual consent, the marriage will not take place. No further explanation is appropriate or necessary. If time is too short to notify the guests by mail, ask a few friends to organize a "telephoning committee."

A similar newspaper announcement may be made. If your parents issued the previous announcement and invitations, they will also issue this "by mutual consent" cancellation announcement.

Return all wedding and shower gifts to the donors. Include a short, personal note along these lines:

"Bob and I have agreed to cancel plans to marry. I am returning to you the beautiful salad bowl you sent us. Once again, I thank you for your generosity and thoughtfulness."

Cancel reservations, appointments and services.

Privately admit to yourself, and enjoy the realization, that it is "better before than after."

Put this book in a safe place to use later at a happier time.

Getting Started

Allow as much time as you can for this section. Every step you take early will not have to be taken later—in the days when parties and showers abound. As you complete an item and record the relevant data, or decide it does not apply to your plan, *check off* the item on the Master Checklist and forget it.

BRIDAL CONSULTANTS

After you have decided the kind of wedding you will have, you might ask, "Do I need a consultant?" That depends solely upon you, your temperament, your schedule and pressures, your parents or available assistance.

Most couples prefer to go through the process of investigating on their own and then, with this book to guide them, attend to the many details themselves. When they make their personal choices, they feel they have achieved a wedding uniquely their own.

There are situations, however, in which a competent consultant or coordinator is not only a boon but a necessity. Engaging the right one for *you* becomes a very personal choice because you will work together closely and must "click." There can be no opposing goals or ideas; your tastes must jell, or at the very least the consultant should *completely understand* what you like.

You need to consider whether you would like a consultant/coordinator who will take *full charge* of everything from start to finish, or one who will assist to a *limited degree* in the particular areas you specify.

Full Charge

An expert full-charge consultant can personally direct the logistics and take responsibility for every phase of the preparations, including the important wedding day itself.

* She has often encountered and solved the same problems that are new and worrisome to you.

* She will know which of the many caterers, photographers, bakers, florists and other services are dependable and efficient, and will engage them.

* She will even take charge of ordering, addressing and sending invitations and announcements.

* Should you need a reception location, she can provide a list that includes cost of rental, capacity, available equipment, parking facilities and liquor

restrictions. She will make arrangements for the one you select.

◆ Most self-employed consultants have imagination and a flair for entertaining. Just as restaurants vary in quality and expertise, so do consultant/coordinators. Only you can judge whether you are on the same wavelength.

Limited Assistance

Some coordinators are primarily caterers who have expanded their contacts in order to fulfill some of their clients' other requirements. They will have available dishes, glassware, silver, chafing dishes and other serving needs. They should be able to oversee the reception routine.

A few major stores and some bridal shops provide consultants who coordinate the wedding party gowns, including that of the mother of the bride. They will help the bride and groom select and register gifts from the store's selection and will have useful suggestions based on their experiences with many engaged couples. Occasionally they will deliver the gown on the wedding day and help the bride dress. A store consultant rarely handles all the services you will need.

Consultant/Coordinator Cost

Before determining cost, you must be aware of how diverse consultant/coordinator services are.

One coordinator might specialize in the-sky's-the-limit excellence, while another takes pride in her economy, even to making available rental wedding gowns. This is why it is essential that you discuss your financial limits frankly. If one consultant is not able to produce what you want within your allotment, consult another.

Charges are made in a variety of ways:

- A flat fee. Inquire exactly what the fee includes and omits.

- A percentage, ranging from 10 percent up to 40 percent, is added on to the bills for services, in which case she will submit the bills to you.

- A fee plus a commission paid directly from the various suppliers she engages.

- An in-house consultant is paid by the establishment for which she works.

You may be wondering whether a consultant is merely a luxury or a necessity. You must interview the consultants in depth, and secure reliable recommendations, before you select one with whom you can work congenially. I strongly recommend that you talk to people who have used the services of the one you are considering. Were they truly satisfied? You might also want to talk to people who did *not* use a consultant. How did they manage?

After you have done your homework, you will know if a consultant is for you.

(For additional information, please see pages 188 to 189.)

SETTING THE DATE AND HOUR

If your budget is tight, remember that an afternoon reception does not call for as expensive a menu as at other times of the day. If you are trying to minimize expenses, select the time that requires the least amount of food and service.

The Wedding Breakfast

The "breakfast" is, in fact, lunch. It takes place after a morning or noon ceremony and may be served at tables—usually three courses—or from a buffet with a number of selections. Drinks may be served before lunch, in addition to wine with lunch and champagne at cake-cutting time.

Afternoon Reception

A tea or cocktail menu, with the addition of a wedding cake, is appropriate. Make it as simple or elaborate as you want—from punch, pretty homemade open-faced sandwiches and wedding cake, to a catered repast of hot and cold canapés, choice of drinks, a buffet of substantial, elegant selections and wedding cake. Even on the tightest budget, it costs nothing to make everything appetizingly attractive. You can rent or borrow plates, but do not settle for paper ones.

Without a doubt, an afternoon wedding when no one expects substantial food can be the least expensive.

A fine and perfect wedding can be produced "on a shoestring" when friends help. In place of hired waiters or waitresses, preteen and early-teenage children of friends pass the platters of goodies. The youngsters, dressed in their best outfits, feel honored, and so do the guests. Some friends will contribute flowers; others will provide dainty sandwiches. Yes, it can be done beautifully though economically if need be. When friends band together to make the day special for you, their warmth does indeed make your unforgettable day even more exceptional.

Dinner

A *late*-afternoon reception may be prolonged until a dinner or supper is served, either at tables or from a buffet. Today, people usually expect that a ceremony later than four o'clock will include dinner or a buffet reception, although this is an extra expense and not necessary.

A dinner requires arranging the seating with place cards. If the guest list is large, seating charts with names in large print are provided along with individual cards indicating table numbers at which the guests place themselves. The person in charge of the guest book distributes these cards at the reception. With a large crowd you may, of course, use individual place cards—a daunting task! This detailed placing of guests is time-consuming and not much fun, but makes each guest feel specially considered.

At a large dinner you might find it preferable to place congenial friends together, while at the smaller rehearsal dinner you intentionally intermingle your guests.

Evening Reception

This is similar to the afternoon reception, following an evening ceremony. Frequently a late supper is served, especially if guests stay for dancing.

Music and Dancing

There need be no music at all at the reception, although this is the exception rather than the rule. If you want music, however, it can be anything from one piece—a piano, accordion or zither—to two dance bands. Popular recently are the less expensive DJs who produce amazing music and sound effects.

It should be noted here that if your reception is to be in a private home, there might be objections from neighbors over the loudness of the music. A safeguard against this, although not foolproof, is graciously to advise each neighbor of the wedding and the time you plan for the music to end. Some brides have even been known to invite every neighbor to come! Advising your local police department of the wedding and when it is planned to end is another nonfoolproof safeguard.

RESERVING A VENUE FOR THE WEDDING CEREMONY

Because there are many edifices in which to worship or be married—temples, cathedrals, synagogues, chapels, etc.—I have used one word, "church," throughout this book to include them all. In addition, one can be married in a home, hotel, garden, club or hall.

I have also used one word, "clergyman," to cover the officials of all denominations, whether they be priest, rabbi, minister, pastor or other. One can also be married by a judge, governor, chaplain or registrar, to name a few.

If your heart is set on a special venue, *reserve it the minute you become engaged!* Weddings are being planned further and further ahead these days; in fact, one woman I know quietly engaged the church before the groom had popped the question! If you wish to be married in a church, when you reserve it be sure to check the availability of the clergyman, as well as the reception hall if you wish to use it.

In the back of this book and in your other wedding records, you will need to note the following information about the ceremony:

- The name and phone number of your clergyman

- The correct full name of the church (for the invitations)

- The church's address and phone number

- The day, date and hour of the ceremony

- The time and date of the rehearsal

- The time to arrive at the church on the wedding day

Descriptions of the rituals and requirements of various denominations have been intentionally omitted from this book. You will either already know the necessary specifics that apply to *your* ceremony, or you will learn about them from your clergyman.

The bride and groom's prime priority is an early first conference with the clergyman of his or her church. If neither of you has a church affiliation, don't set your heart on your wedding taking place in one particular church until after you confer. Even within the same denomination one finds clergymen with differing attitudes, interpretations and regulations. For this reason all your wedding plans will depend on *who* will officiate—and *where*.

DISCUSSION WITH THE CLERGYMAN

The following items need to be covered:

- Do you need to obtain a DISPENSATION, or permission to marry, in case of divorce or a mixed marriage?

- Are there RESTRICTIONS for the day of the week or ecclesiastical season in which you may marry?

- Any RESTRICTIONS regarding attendants' religions?

- Does the church require PREMARITAL CONFERENCES, or attendance over a period of time, before your marriage? Some churches now mandate a six-month or more preparation period.

- If you and your husband-to-be are of DIFFERENT FAITHS, you may want to ask if a clergyman representing each of your faiths may officiate jointly. They often do.

- Can you obtain approval if you wish to incorporate special or PERSONALLY WRITTEN VOWS? Not all clergymen will consent.

- Ascertain the FORM AND LENGTH OF SERVICE.

- Secure permission from the clergyman for a soloist, choir or other MUSIC OR PERFORMERS OF YOUR CHOICE.

- Some couples MEMORIZE THEIR VOWS and speak them instead of repeating the clergyman's statements. "Speaking" is delightful only when done easily; it is painful to hear when, under tension, the vows come out whispered, or garbled. Unless you are confident that you will both—repeat *both*—be comfortable and relaxed, stay with a conventional exchange of vows. They are lovely.

- A voluntary HONORARIUM will be paid to the clergyman on the day of the ceremony; this is the groom's responsibility.

MAKE CHURCH ARRANGEMENTS

All but the smallest of churches will have a secretary, and in addition many will have a wedding coordinator. Either one is well versed in everything that takes place within the church and will advise you on all the following details:

- PAYMENT for the sexton, and the organist if provided by the church, as well as other charges.

- Are any specific MUSICAL NUMBERS BANNED?

- RULES REGARDING PHOTOGRAPHY AND VIDEO recording inside the church.

- FACILITIES for the bridal party to freshen up, or to dress if they have to drive a great distance.

- Where the bridal party should PARK.

- DECORATIONS: any restrictions regarding flowers or candles?

- Is there a wedding scheduled immediately before or after yours? Sometimes the secretary or church wedding coordinator will put the two brides in touch, so that they may cooperate in planning and SHARING THE COST OF DECORATIONS. (Be sure there is ample time between the two weddings, however; the earlier wedding could run a bit late and guests could begin to arrive early for the second wedding.)

- Does the church provide a KNEELING CUSHION? A CANVAS RUNNER? A WEDDING CEREMONY PROGRAM?

- Some churches provide a COMMUNITY ROOM in which to hold the reception. If you are interested, check on the details listed in the following section on venues for wedding receptions.

- Keep in mind that you will probably be INVITING THE OFFICIATING CLERGYMAN, his wife and the wedding coordinator of the church to the reception.

RESERVING A VENUE FOR
THE RECEPTION

You might wonder how to find a reception locale to fit
your specifications. The search is especially difficult if
you are from out of town. Recommendations from
friends are always helpful. Websites, bookstores and li-
braries stock guides for local sites. The chamber of
commerce and business associations also have pertinent information, or can refer you to other sources. A
telephone call will elicit some cold facts, such as cost
and capacity, but *be sure* to visit in person to see if the
accommodations appeal to you.

You may decide to hold your wedding reception at
any number of venues, including the same place your
wedding ceremony was performed. When you are deciding the location, keep in mind to expect that 75 percent of those you invite will attend. If the reception is
to be held in your home (or a friend's), begin now to
plan for the garden, house décor and cleaning of the
house before the reception. If it is to be held at a hotel,
restaurant or club, make the reservation now. You can
take care of the final details later.

If you plan to be married out of town or at a family-
only affair, the reception may be held at a later date.
Either set of parents or the bridal couple themselves
may give it. This delayed reception is usually more informal and follows a tea or cocktail party plan. *(See
pages 19 to 25.)*

If you plan to hold the reception in a church community room, find out exactly what equipment is provided: stove and oven, coffeemakers, refrigeration, china, glasses? Important: inquire about possible restrictions as to alcoholic beverages.

Reception halls are available, especially in or near large cities. Many are equipped to provide everything—a complete package. "Everything" can include rooms in which to dress, flowers, photographers, refreshments, even someone to officiate at the ceremony, if desired. Such halls often have a variety of banquet rooms to accommodate any number of people, and they offer anything from a simple tea menu to an elaborate dinner. As with all services, you will find a wide range of price and quality.

Getting Your Team in Place

Planning a wedding is a group effort, and here's where you start getting the members of your team on board.

In your wedding computer program/notebook/file (whichever method suits you), you will need a section on "Services." Here you will put the names, addresses, phone numbers, e-mails and faxes of the florist, caterer, photographer and others. Keep in mind that it is helpful if this information can be readily available to more than one person. For easy reference, there is a section in this book called "Important Contacts," where you will record information about your team members. *(See pages 227 to 230.)*

ENGAGING A CATERER

If your reception is to be held at a hotel or club, the catering department will provide all the necessities you want and need, but if the reception is at home or in a rented hall, you will have to make your own arrangements for food and service. Whether or not you use a caterer depends on you.

The factors to consider are the number of guests, time of day, location, customs of your community and expense. You will be ready to make your decision after you read the following information.

What a Caterer Can Provide

A competent caterer will provide the food and an adequate staff of cooks, waiters or waitresses, and bartenders. He prepares much of the food in his own kitchen. If kitchen facilities at the reception venue are limited, he can transport hot food in portable ovens. He can supply glasses, dishes, tea service, punch bowls, tables, table linens, chairs—almost everything you want.

Most caterers are experienced in what they call "circulation" for serving, and in receiving line procedure. Discuss your reception with him in detail. He has been responsible for a multitude and variety of parties, so take advantage of his knowledge. If you have a receiving line, he might be able to suggest a previously unthought of location for it, in order to relieve congestion. There is no law that says the bride *must* receive in front of the fireplace—especially if that position would hamper circulation. Here are some interesting variations:

- Set up a tent. Portable heaters do wonders for a tented area.

- Transform a two-car garage into a temporary party room and receive there. Yes, a garage! You have only to remove bicycles, paint cans and other clutter, and start decorating. Cover the floors with a borrowed or rented rug; for tables, set up sawhorses topped with planks or a door and cover them with pretty cloths or satin yardage; rent espaliered trees or shrubs for a beautiful background.

- You might decide to have some of the furniture removed from the house and held overnight in a moving van. This would enable you to use floor space freely. Perhaps you will dance in the dining room and dine in the living room.

- Some caterers are qualified to handle the decorating and arrange for music, flowers and other special services, if you wish.

- Some caterers can act as major-domo/master of ceremonies, or they can offer the services of a hostess who will keep the reception routine flowing smoothly.

Deciding on the Best Caterer

Depend heavily upon strong recommendations from people whose style you admire and respect. Rarely—but occasionally—one hears of a caterer who underestimated quantity and ran out of food with fifty guests yet to be served. Horrible thought!

How a Caterer Charges

A catering firm will arrive at the total charge by adding together the cost of the following items and submitting a contract for you to sign.

- Either the total cost of food plus an agreed-upon percentage *or*, more often, the cost of each serving or dinner multiplied by the number of guests—known as the charge per head. Your menu choices will govern the cost.

- Charges for the staff's working time.

- Rental charges for dishes, glasses and other equipment you request.

- Other specified services or provisions, such as music, decorations, drinks, wedding cake.

The caterer will estimate from his own experience the number of waiters or waitresses he needs for your reception. To ensure excellent service, I always ask the caterer to engage extra help. A bit extravagant, but you might decide it is worth the extra—just this once!

At the original consultation you can roughly estimate the number of guests. The contract will state a cut-off date for specifying a firm number.

Most caterers will submit a bill after the reception takes place. Pay it promptly. Some caterers will request a sizable advance payment; others ask for full payment in advance. I would never engage the latter caterer.

Canceling a Contract

If, due to an emergency, you have to call off or postpone the wedding, what is your obligation? A contract is an agreement to pay regardless of personal problems. If you cancel far enough ahead, however, you might be granted some leniency. Leniency depends on the caterer's attitude and often on his relationship with a customer. If you are a good customer, he will probably take that into consideration. If it is too late to place the staff elsewhere, you will be fully obligated to pay. If he has not yet purchased the food, he might relieve you of that expense.

Caterers who are also in the restaurant business are often able to use the food, even if you cancel late; if they cannot use it, they will charge you.

Other Catering Considerations

If you do decide to hire a caterer, be sure you have made a future date together to discuss final details—at least two weeks before the wedding, preferably sooner.

Whether you engage a caterer, hire your own help or use the assistance of kind friends, you need to make decisions about all the following items. Cross off those items that do not apply to your plan.

♦ THE WEDDING CAKE: WHO WILL FURNISH IT? Prices, workmanship, quality and taste vary considerably. What kind of DECORATION do you want? Consider substituting flowers made of icing for the little bride-and-groom figures so often seen atop cakes. Better still might be real flowers in a tiny glass set into the top of the cake. Look up nonpoisonous varieties of flowers. Fresh flowers can also be used spilling out between the cake tiers. Sparkling crystal decorations, while ruinous to your bankbook, are exquisite to behold. What FLAVOR cake do you want? In the past, all wedding cakes were fruitcake, but today one may chose whatever flavors one likes, even with a different flavor for each tier! Traditionally the top tier is saved in the freezer to be enjoyed on your first anniversary.

Some brides also chose an additional, smaller cake, called the GROOM'S CAKE, in a flavor that the groom particularly enjoys. It may be placed near the wedding cake or on a separate table.

In the past, BOXED INDIVIDUAL SLICES of wedding cake were passed out to the wedding guests to take home. Today this is unexpected and an unnecessary luxury.

- MENU: This, of course, depends on the type of reception you are planning.

- NAPKINS: Do you want them PRINTED with the bride and groom's names or initials and the date? Matchbooks can be printed also, but with the decline of smoking, now they are often filled with a mini-notepad instead.

- TABLES AND CHAIRS.

- GLASSES.

- DISHES.

- PUNCH BOWL.

- FLATWARE.

- SERVING PLATTERS.

- BEVERAGES: Will you have an OPEN, FULL BAR, or will you serve ONLY BEER AND WINE or soft drinks and waters?

- TUBS TO ICE CHAMPAGNE: You can chill large quantities in the tub of your washing machine. Afterward simply drain or spin out the melted ice, or add water and detergent to soak dish towels and napkins.

- LOCATION OF SERVING CENTERS FOR FOOD AND DRINKS.

- GUEST BOOK TABLE.

- RICE, CONFETTI, ROSE PETALS OR BIRDSEED: to shower the departing couple. While you are changing, little packets or baskets of rice, confetti, rose petals or birdseed may be passed to the guests. (Some of the very young would love this assignment.) Remember that rice can sting faces and make stairs dangerously slippery, and rose petals stain rugs. Paper rose petals are available at wedding supply shops and are a good choice; confetti rates second best. The ecology-minded opt for birdseed—out of doors, of course. I know of at least one bride who opted to use little decorated bottles of bubble mix with wands to blow bubbles at the couple and save that entire cleanup! Before you make a choice or go to the trouble of making or ordering the packets, check with the reception locale management. Hotels and clubs seldom permit the use of rice, and sometimes forbid throwing *anything*. You have freedom of choice only if your reception is at home.

- ◆ ICE.

- ◆ Where will EXTRA STAFF be needed? Will you want them at the door to take wraps? To pass refreshments?

- ◆ COAT RACKS AND HANGERS.

- ◆ WHO WILL MOVE FURNITURE before and after the reception?

- ◆ An ALTERNATE RAIN PLAN.

- ◆ FOOD AND SOFT DRINKS FOR THE BAND.

THE FLORIST

Flowers are an integral part of any wedding, and a talented friend or a competent, well-recommended florist may do them. As soon as you have a wedding date, it is advisable for you to arrange for a florist, or someone, to do the flowers at the wedding and the reception. Make an appointment for a consultation as soon as possible, and take this book with you to discuss all the points listed below.

- ◆ CHURCH DECORATIONS: On occasion, after the ceremony the florist can transport some of the flowers from the church and add them to the reception decorations. A further thought: If another wedding is scheduled to precede or follow yours in the church, you might investigate sharing the cost, provided your tastes are similar.

- ◆ RECEPTION DECORATIONS.

- ◆ DECORATION FOR THE WEDDING CAKE TABLE: Other than the decorations on the cake itself, you may want some extra flowers on the table. One lovely way, and economical, is to use the table as a depository for the bridesmaids' bouquets during the reception. This makes an attractive presentation, and gives the bridesmaids a place to lay their bouquets while dancing. An easy-to-forget detail is that someone must be designated to remind the bridesmaids to do so! Of course, the bridesmaids should retrieve their bouquets at the end of the reception.

- ◆ WHITE SATIN RIBBONS AND FLOWERS FOR THE CAKE KNIFE.

- ◆ Small flowers tied with white ribbon on STEMS OF TOASTING GLASSES.

- **BRIDE'S BOUQUET:** Discuss what will be suitable with the gown. Proportion is important. Some brides choose to carry a white prayer book without flowers or with a marker of satin ribbons and flowers.

- **BRIDE'S GOING-AWAY CORSAGE:** This is optional, especially as some brides these days do not change clothes at all and choose to leave the reception in their wedding dress.

- **FLOWERS FOR THE BRIDE'S MOTHER, GROOM'S MOTHER AND GRANDMOTHERS:** Currently, most mothers prefer nosegays and grandmothers prefer corsages.

- **BOUTONNIERES** for ushers, groomsmen, best man, groom, fathers and ring bearer. Be sure to designate someone to pass them out to the men, as these flowers are easily lost in the shuffle, especially if the men arrive separately at the wedding.

- **FLOWERS FOR THE BRIDE'S ATTENDANTS:** Costly varieties of flowers are less important than styling, proportion and color.

- **TIME AND PLACE OF DELIVERY:** Be very clear where the flowers are to be delivered, and remember they need to be delivered in time for photographs; chart with your florist the time and place of delivery for the bridal party, the mothers' flowers, the men's boutonnieres and the grandmothers' corsages.

- A CANVAS RUNNER for the center aisle: This is optional, but the florist will provide it if your church does not.

If you intend to do your own decorating, don't leave it until the wedding day.

There is a popular misconception that the term "fresh flowers" means they are arranged immediately after they are cut. According to the experts, flowers and greenery are fresher and last longer after they have been hardened.

To harden: Strip the stems of all leaves that will be in the water; submerge the stem ends and cut to the desired length under water. This method will prevent air pockets from forming and will encourage the intake of water.

Soak greenery in deep water for at least a day; soak flowers for at least several hours after you make the new cut. Keep in a cool place.

Note: In the past it has been customary for the groom to pay for the bride's bouquet, flowers for the mothers, and boutonnieres for the ushers, best man, ring bearer and himself. He *may* pay for the attendants' flowers, and the going-away corsage if there is one. This is a nice custom, but it is entirely optional.

PHOTOGRAPHS AND VIDEOTAPES

The permanent record of your ceremony and reception is next in importance to the wedding itself. You will look at the photographs or watch the videotapes over and over again during your lifetime. You might start a tradition of viewing your pictures on each anniversary date. It is almost like renewing your vows.

Brides are often surprised and distressed to find that the photographer of their choice was booked months ago, and they must settle for fourth or fifth choice. Investigate, then engage your photographer or video service (or both) as soon as you possibly can.

+ Engage a photographer who is a SPECIALIST IN WED-DINGS: An excellent portrait photographer is not necessarily adept at handling group pictures or candid shots discreetly. A specialist is familiar with wedding procedure and timing. He will anticipate the bridal couple's next move and will be in the proper place at the proper time.

+ A clear understanding of WHAT THE PHOTOGRA-PHER WILL DO is essential. Ask your friends for their recommendations.

+ Ask to SEE A PHOTOGRAPHER'S FINISHED WORK before you make a final decision.

+ Make sure YOU can SELECT THE PICTURES for the albums.

- Be certain you will have a SUFFICIENT NUMBER OF PROOFS to allow an adequate selection. Several hundred is not too many.

- Make certain the photographer will take all the SPECIAL PICTURES you request.

- The FEE is partially based upon the time required. To avoid misunderstandings and consequent disappointment, specify enough time for him to stay throughout the reception.

- Get a FIRM PRICE IN WRITING on pictures and albums.

- HOW MANY PICTURES will be included in the album?

- What is the COST OF EXTRA PRINTS? Extra albums for parents?

- Does the photographer require a DOWN PAYMENT?

- Will he submit the proofs and deliver the FINISHED PHOTOGRAPHS BEFORE YOU MAKE THE FINAL PAYMENT?

- When will the PROOFS be submitted?

- When can you expect the FINISHED PHOTOGRAPHS?

- Will he OBJECT TO CANDID SHOTS SNAPPED BY ENTHUSIASTIC FRIENDS? He should not object; the candids will not replace his work.

- **REQUEST "NO SUBSTITUTE."** When you are in complete agreement, make it clear you wish to engage the specific photographer whose portfolio you like, not the studio.

- Arrange a **TIME AND PLACE FOR YOUR FORMAL BRIDAL PORTRAIT**, if you desire one. Some fine gown salons provide space for this at the time of the final fitting, or your photographer may request you come to his studio. If you wait to have your portrait taken on your wedding day, however, the wedding bouquet will be your own, your gown will not have to be transported to the studio—*and*—everyone knows a bride is *always* most beautiful on her wedding day.

- Give the photographer a **LIST OF PICTURES YOU MUST HAVE.** In addition to the standard high points such as cutting the cake and toasting, you will want pictures such as the groom's parents with the bride and groom, the girl with the guest book, and candids of certain relatives, school groups and friends. It is a good idea to ask a responsible friend to stay with the photographer long enough to point out those people.

- Arrange to take as many **PHOTOGRAPHS** as possible **BEFORE** THE WEDDING ceremony. There is nothing worse for your guests than an interminable wait outside the church while photographs are being taken after the ceremony. Many of today's brides have given up the custom of the groom's seeing her the first time in her wedding dress as she comes down the aisle. The photographer and others may give the bride and groom a moment alone before the wedding as they meet for the first time in their wedding finery; the photographs may then be taken and the bridal party will arrive promptly at the reception following the ceremony.

+ Will you VIDEOTAPE your wedding? Videotaping of weddings is quite popular, although increasingly brides are opting not to have it done, as the video cameras are obtrusive. If you chose to do so, investigate thoroughly (as with the photographer) levels of experience and service to assure getting exactly what you want. You may opt for anything from an unedited ceremony-only tape, produced by a single camera, to the ultimate of a highly edited daylong production with two or more cameras in action. There are a number of variations between these two, and the price scale ranges accordingly.

+ Set the EXACT TIME for the photographer or videotaper to be at the church, or whatever venue you have chosen for your pre-ceremony photographs. Be sure to ascertain the church rules regarding picture taking. Some churches forbid it; others specify which studios they favor—based upon the photographers' previous restrained manners.

+ REMIND THE PHOTOGRAPHERS AND VIDEOTAPERS TO BE DISCREET: There should be no dashing down the aisle in pursuit of a picture . . . and a camera should *never* be permitted in the chancel, on the rail or near the altar. To do this would spoil the beauty and solemnity of your perfect wedding.

- OBTAIN PERMISSION in advance from the club or hotel's board of directors or manager. Some venues have rules and restrictions about videotaping because of the need to set up cables and lighting.

- Confirm with the photographer/videotaper WHAT HE PLANS TO WEAR to the wedding. Professionals will wear clothes that blend with the guests' attire.

- A PHOTOGRAPHER MUST NEVER ADVERTISE at your wedding. A photographer may certainly give a guest his business card, if requested, but should never display advertising, even on his lapel.

- Instruct the photographer NOT TO HOLD UP THE RE-CEIVING LINE, if you have opted to have one, by taking too many pictures while guests are waiting. Your photographer has heard this many, many times. Tell him again, and mean it.

- Give the photographer a written LIST OF NEWSPA-PERS to which he should send your favorite glossy prints, with deadlines. Send different poses if the newspapers are located in towns close to each other. If your photographer does not provide this service, you may do this yourself after contacting the papers to determine their requirements.

- REMIND YOUR PHOTOGRAPHER TO BE DISCREET.

The best photographers are invisible. I have often seen a happy time-marred by obtrusive, bossy and officious photographers who are more interested in their own agenda than yours. Be *insistent*! Remember, it is *your* wedding.

Sometimes a nonprofessional friend will offer to record your day on film. He might plan to make this your wedding present—and a fine one indeed! If you accept his generosity, supply him with film, and give him an important gift afterward. For a large wedding, however, a nonprofessional photographer would not be as satisfactory. You might be reluctant to give a friend who donates his services the same instructions you would give a person you pay.

MUSIC FOR THE WEDDING

You will have determined at your church conference if you are required to use a church-provided organist (whom you will pay) or if you may engage outside musicians. You will also have been informed if certain musical numbers are not permitted.

If you wish to have a soloist, choir or other special music at your ceremony, a good time to do this is immediately before the processional if the ceremony is short, or while a Communion or other service is being prepared if the ceremony is long. You may, of course, choose any time you wish during the ceremony for your personal music selections.

Make sure the musicians are familiar with the selections you request and when they are to perform them.

Make a note of the musicians' names and arrange for payment before or after the wedding day, if possible. It is distracting to have to write checks on the day of the wedding, but if you must, try to write them beforehand and ask the best man to pass them out.

MUSIC FOR THE RECEPTION

There need be no music at all at the reception. If you want music, however, it can be anything from one piece—a piano, guitar, accordion or zither—to a DJ or two dance bands. After you have decided on your musicians, make notes of who they are and arrange for making payment either before or after the reception.

You will need to attend to the following:

- WHAT WILL THE MUSICIANS WEAR?

- Set an exact TIME FOR THE MUSICIANS' ARRIVAL at the reception. Determine what gear the musicians will want to deliver ahead of time (speakers, instruments, staging, etc.) and make pertinent arrangements.

- Arrange for a SPECIAL FANFARE to announce the cake cutting and any other happening, such as the toast from the best man.

- Well in advance, give the leader a LIST OF THE BRIDE AND GROOM'S FAVORITE SELECTIONS for both background and dance music.

- If there is to be no dancing, the musicians will play BACKGROUND MUSIC ONLY.

- If there is to be dancing, the musicians will play BACKGROUND MUSIC until the dancing begins.

- Discuss your DANCE SEQUENCE. It is an old tradition that no one should dance until the bride and groom have had the first dance, frequently a waltz. Following this, there is a dance order that you may choose to follow if you keep this tradition:

  * *First dance:* bride and groom alone.

  * *Second dance:* bride and her father; groom and bride's mother.

  * *Third dance:* Bride and groom; bride's father and groom's mother; bride's mother and groom's father; ushers and bridesmaids. Then everyone dances, and anyone may cut in and dance with the bride, always festive and fun.

Arranging the Wedding Party

SELECTING YOUR BRIDAL PARTY

Well in advance of the wedding, you will want to select your bridesmaids and maid or matron of honor, and your fiancé his ushers and best man (groomsmen). The number of attendants is your decision, although a very large number of attendants would not be appropriate at a small wedding. One usher is needed for every fifty guests. It is not necessary to have the same number of bridesmaids as ushers.

It sets a positive family tone for the bride and groom's siblings to be asked to be attendants, and it is not unusual for the groom to ask his father to be best man. The rest of the wedding party may consist of close friends and relatives. I recently attended a wedding where the bride had her three brothers as attendants, and another where the "best man" was a woman. Most important, you must be sure that your attendants are reliable and truly interested in helping to make this a happy wedding for you and your fiancé.

Select your bridesmaids from among your close

friends. Don't choose your maid or matron of honor from "among the ranks." Decide whom you want in advance, then invite her specifically for this special position. If a bridesmaid (or usher) has to drop out at the last minute, do not attempt to find a replacement. The substitute might wonder why he or she was not invited in the first place. Uneven numbers are quite acceptable in the processional and recessional—sometimes even by prearrangement—this isn't Noah's Ark.

Many people of experience advise against including a flower girl or ring bearer in the wedding party. Children are notorious scene-stealers. By all means include them, however, if your heart is set on it and you are willing to risk scene-stealing on your big day.

Keep in mind the duties of the members of the bridal party as you invite each one to participate, and choose accordingly. A best man who is interested only in a good party would not be a good choice! The following are the duties of members of the bridal party. To make sure they are informed, it might be a good idea to give each a copy of these pages.

The male members of the wedding party are sometimes referred to as "groomsmen." This term refers to *all* of the male members of the wedding party, i.e., best man *and* ushers. Ushers alone should not be referred to as "groomsmen."

The Best Man

The best man is an extra pair of legs and an extra head for the groom. His responsibilities are many, varied and important, and he must do whatever he can to cooperate with and assist the groom. If the best man is from out of town, some of these responsibilities can be managed by the head usher. Occasionally, but not customarily, a groom *invites his father to serve as best man.*

If outfits for the groom and men of the wedding party are rented, it is the best man's responsibility **to** *pick the suits up and return them* after the wedding, being sure to check all pockets for personal belongings. Each man will pay for the rental of his own outfit.

Occasionally the groom will *purchase ties and gloves* for the men in the bridal party. If this is the case, the best man may assist by determining the men's glove sizes and buying them for him.

Sometimes the groomsmen host the bachelor dinner. The best man can *help organize both the dinner and finances.* Other times the groom gives this party. If so, the best man can *make the reservations for him, help select the menu and drinks, and see that the ushers know the time and place.*

The ushers and best man customarily *purchase a gift for the groom.* The best man may organize this effort.

He may help the groom with *honeymoon reservations* if necessary. If the bridal couple plan to stay in a nearby hotel after the wedding, they can be preregistered, then go directly to their room.

The best man can *register at the hotel* for them and bring the key to the groom, swearing on his honor not to divulge their plans!

Although there is usually a head usher, the best man

is *in charge of all the ushers*. He reminds them *where* to be, and *when*, for the parties, rehearsal, the ceremony and the reception.

The bride and groom might wish to hide the honeymoon car, in which case the best man can *place their luggage in the car* ahead of time. When they leave the reception, he drives them to their car, unless a taxi or limousine has been ordered.

On the wedding day, the best man will *help the groom dress*. He should check out the groom's and his own clothes and accessories well before that day. He should put everything—studs, shirt, tie—in one place. This is especially important if he is dressing elsewhere. He also *takes the wedding ring to the church* in a safe pocket or on his little finger, if it will fit.

The best man *makes sure the groom has obtained the wedding license*. The best man takes it to the church himself. After the wedding, the license must be signed by the clergyman and witnesses, most likely the best man and maid of honor.

The best man *pays the clergyman*. The groom will give him an envelope with the honorarium inside. He pays the clergyman quietly in the vestry, either before the ceremony or after while he witnesses the signing of the marriage certificate.

The best man *gives the first toast* to the bride, usually just before the cake is cut.

Immediately after toasting the bride, *he reads some messages* that may have arrived from those unable to attend the wedding.

He *dances with the bride, the mothers and the bridesmaids.*

If the groom's father serves as best man, a few of the duties listed here can be taken over by the head usher.

As you can see, the best man is of tremendous assistance to the groom, who definitely has other things on his mind.

Head Usher

Consider selecting a head usher, who has some important responsibilities. *He helps the best man with his many duties,* especially if he is local and the best man is from out of town. Additionally, because the best man is not available during the seating of guests at the ceremony, the head usher will *manage the other ushers* in matters including: seating of special pew-card holders, arranging the canvas runner and ushering family members before and after the ceremony.

Ushers

The ushers have been selected because they are the groom's close friends. In that capacity as honored and special friends, they add much geniality to pre-wedding and wedding reception festivities. For the wedding itself, their duties are specific.

Ushers *pay for their own rental outfits.* The groom will tell them where he has made the arrangements for the rental. Each usher should go as soon as possible to have his measurements taken, and go later for his fitting when scheduled.

Ushers, as a group, *give the groom a memento*. One popular gift is a silver box engraved with their signatures.

In the festivities preceding the wedding, it is appropriate for unmarried or unattached ushers to offer to *escort bridesmaids to parties*.

Ushers must *attend the wedding rehearsal*—on time.

On the wedding day, ushers should *arrive at the church an hour ahead of time*.

Ushers' *boutonnieres are pinned on the left lapel*; the buttonhole is only decorative.

Each usher *offers his right arm to each woman guest and escorts her to a pew*. He asks if she is a friend of the bride or groom, seating the bride's friends on the left of the aisle, the groom's on the right. As the church fills, it may be necessary to balance the number of guests on either side of the aisle. He should simply ask the guests if they would mind. The men and children in the escorted guest's group follow them to the pew. The same procedure is followed with unaccompanied men, but the usher does not offer his arm.

The head usher *seats the mother of the groom*. Her husband follows a few steps behind.

The head usher *escorts the mother of the bride to her pew*. She is the last person to be seated. If her son is an usher, he may escort his mother if she prefers. At one wedding I attended, the mother of the bride was escorted by *two* sons who were ushers—a meaningful variation.

At a very formal wedding a *white canvas runner* furnished by the church or the florist *may be laid on the center aisle*. If the runner is in place ahead of time, the ushers escort guests to their pews from the side aisles. At other times the runner is placed by two ushers after the mother of the bride is seated.

Ushers must *familiarize themselves with the special pew holders' seating plan.*

If the church has a balcony, an usher will be assigned to seat guests there. Since late-arriving guests will probably be seated in the balcony, it is a good idea to assign someone else to seat them so the usher may join in the processional.

Two or more ushers may be asked to *return after the recessional to escort the bride's and groom's mothers and grandmothers out of the church*. More often, the bride's mother and father lead the way, followed by the groom's parents; the guests follow, alternating left and right, row by row.

The ushers are responsible for *transporting (or escorting, if limousines have been hired) the bridesmaids from the church to the reception,* promptly.

Occasionally an usher is asked to *substitute for an announcer in the receiving line,* if the bride and groom have chosen to have a receiving line. As announcer, he merely asks the guest's name and repeats it to the first person in the receiving line.

Genial though they may be, ushers should be aware that *mild practical jokes can be funny as long as they do not embarrass, endanger or disrupt.*

Bridesmaids

Bridesmaids have an important role. What could be more reassuring to the bride than knowing she is surrounded by her closest friends who will support her before, during and after her wedding! Bridesmaids bring their gaiety, beauty and the warmest of feelings to the wedding and reception.

Bridesmaids often *plan a shower or other party* for the bride.

They *have their gowns fitted on schedule.*

They *join in the prenuptial party time.*

When The Important Day arrives, they *walk down the aisle* with happy and relaxed smiles.

Maid of Honor or Matron of Honor

This honored bridal attendant has more responsibilities than the other bridesmaids do.

She *helps the bride dress* on her wedding day.

She *holds the bride's bouquet, and possibly her gloves,* during the ceremony.

If it is a double-ring ceremony, she *holds the groom's ring.*

If the bride wishes, she *folds back her veil at the altar.*

She *stands in the receiving line* with the other attendants. She can help speed the progress of the line by introducing the next bridesmaid clearly and with pleasure.

After the receiving line dissolves, she *mingles with the guests* and has fun.

She *helps the bride change* from her wedding gown to her going-away outfit.

It is the maid of honor's duty to *inform the parents of the bride and groom* when the newlyweds are ready to leave.

As the best man is *an extra pair of legs and an extra head* for the groom, so is the maid of honor for the bride on her exciting day. She can help smooth the bride's way.

Ring Bearer, Flower Girl and Junior Bridesmaid

The *ring bearer* should wear his best dress-up suit—navy blue, or perhaps white linen in the summer. If purchased, it is paid for by his parents. He carries a white satin, brocade or tapestry pillow with the wedding ring (the real one or a substitute) stitched on.

The *flower girl's* dress, to be paid for by her parents, should harmonize with the bridesmaids' gowns, and her bouquet should be scaled down in size. Instead of a bouquet, the flower girl may carry a basket of paper rose petals to strew along the bride's path.

If the wedding procession includes both a ring bearer and a flower girl, they often precede the bride and her escort in that order. In the recessional they follow the bride and groom and walk side by side.

The flower girl, ring bearer and their parents should be included in all transportation arrangements.

The children probably will be too young to join in the receiving line.

The bride should give each child a keepsake gift and a photograph of the wedding party. They will treasure it.

✓ The parents of the child attendants should be invited to substitute for their children at the rehearsal dinner.

A *junior bridesmaid,* age ten to fourteen, has the same duties and privileges as other bridesmaids. In the processional she follows the maid or matron of honor and precedes the ring bearer and flower girl, if any. In the recessional she walks immediately behind the bride and groom unless there is a flower girl or ring bearer, in which case she follows. Her gown should be modified to suit her age.

RESPONSIBILITIES OF THE GROOM

The groom often has less to think about than the bride does, but he does have definite responsibilities. He must:

- BE PRESENT AT THE CONFERENCE WITH THE CLERGYMAN. Other prenuptial meetings might be required.

- Endear himself to you and his future mother-in-law by BEATING THE DEADLINE FOR TURNING IN HIS AND HIS FAMILY'S GUEST LIST.

- PURCHASE A WEDDING RING FOR THE BRIDE.

- If he wishes, as most grooms do, he will GIVE HIS BRIDE-TO-BE A PERSONAL GIFT, such as a piece of jewelry.

- PURCHASE A PERMANENT KEEPSAKE FOR EACH OF THE USHERS. *(See page 144.)*

- ARRANGE HIS BUSINESS AFFAIRS by drawing up his will, changing the beneficiary on his life insurance and arranging a joint and/or separate bank account.

- MAKE ARRANGEMENTS FOR THE HONEYMOON, for which he pays, traditionally, unless generous parents provide the gift. He must send deposits and make sure he has letters of confirmation. If the bride and groom are planning to stay in a nearby hotel and will arrive late, he may register in advance so you may go directly to your room, or he may ask the best man to help with these arrangements.

- MAKE FINANCIAL ARRANGEMENTS FOR YOUR NEW HOME or apartment, including utilities.

- GET A PHYSICAL CHECKUP, DENTAL CHECKUP AND BLOOD TEST, if your state requires one.

- DISCUSS AND COOPERATE FULLY WITH THE BRIDE CONCERNING WHAT THE MEN IN THE BRIDAL PARTY WILL WEAR AT THE WEDDING. The bride will set the pattern by deciding on the setting, time of day and degree of formality of her wedding gown—all of which establish the type of attire the men should wear. He should not let the rental establishment persuade him to let the groomsmen wear inappropriate suits, such as dinner jackets before six in the evening, or colorful outfits at any time. *(See pages 103 to 105.)* As soon as he and the bride have selected the style, he must RESERVE THE NUMBER OF OUTFITS NEEDED AND ASK THE BEST MAN TO NOTIFY LOCAL USHERS TO GO IMMEDIATELY TO HAVE THEIR MEASUREMENTS TAKEN. For groomsmen who live out of town, the rental establishment will give out measurement cards that the men can have filled out by tailors in their places of residence. The best man must BEG THE GROOMSMEN TO RETURN THE COMPLETED CARDS *PROMPTLY*. The outfits will be reserved for them with preliminary alterations. Last-minute fittings, and adjustments if needed, can be made when the men arrive in town for the wedding.

- If he desires, BUY WEDDING TIES AND GLOVES (if they are to be worn) to present to the ushers and best man as gifts.

- GO WITH THE BRIDE TO GET THE MARRIAGE LICENSE.

- ARRANGE PLACES TO STAY FOR THE OUT-OF-TOWN MEN IN THE WEDDING PARTY. It is nice if local friends or relatives offer to house the groomsmen, but if they don't, the groom should make hotel reservations for them. At one time it was considered the groom's responsibility to pay for the accommodations of his groomsmen; today either way is appropriate.

- **ARRANGE TO BE BILLED BY THE FLORIST FOR CERTAIN OF THE WEDDING FLOWERS.** Grooms do not always choose to do this, although it is a very fine gesture. The groom may pay for the bride's bouquet, flowers for the mothers (today's choice is frequently nosegays) and boutonnieres for himself and the ushers. Going away corsages—once considered a "must"— are out of fashion as of this date (indeed, going-away outfits are not always seen anymore), but styles come and go, and then come again. If corsages are ordered, he should add that to his florist bill. He may also pay for the bridesmaids' bouquets if he wishes, although they are usually considered part of the wedding décor. All flowers are selected by the bride.

- **PAY THE CLERGYMAN'S FEE.** This is actually an honorarium, which the clergyman will keep or donate to the church. The amount is left to the groom's discretion; the more elaborate the wedding, the larger the contribution. New currency should be placed in an envelope and given to the best man, who will hand it to the clergyman in the vestry room, either before the ceremony or immediately after, when the marriage certificate will be signed.

- **GET A HAIRCUT,** but *not* immediately before the wedding in order to avoid that new-shorn look.

- **COORDINATE THE BACHELOR DINNER,** usually arranged by the best man. It may be hosted by the groom or the ushers, and if possible, scheduled early in the week before the wedding. A month or so ahead of the wedding is also fine, if this is the only time when everyone can get together.

- **BLACKEN THE SOLES OF HIS SHOES.** They will look better when he kneels during the ceremony.

- BE OF GOOD CHEER.

THE GROOM'S FAMILY

Because almost all wedding responsibilities and decisions traditionally belong to the bride and her parents, the groom's family may feel superfluous—even the groom feels forgotten at moments during the hectic rush of bridal activities. There is no such thing as a groomless wedding, however—he is indispensable and *so are his parents!*

The groom's parents play an important role at the ceremony and reception as special guests of honor; if they read this book, they will empathize with all the bride must do, and they may follow this chapter for their own list of do's and don'ts. They will feel at ease if they know exactly what is expected of them.

- **THE ENGAGEMENT:** As soon as their son tells them "She said yes," the groom's parents SHOULD TELEPHONE THE BRIDE-TO-BE to express their pleasure that she is going to be their new daughter. This is followed by a telephone call to her parents to arrange to CALL ON THEM OR INVITE THEM TO DINNER. In addition to this, they should WRITE THEM AN ENTHUSIASTIC LETTER, as well as a separate one to the bride.

After the engagement has been announced, the groom's parents might like to GIVE A COCKTAIL PARTY, TEA OR SOME SORT OF FESTIVE GATHERING to introduce the bride to their friends. If not, they may entertain for her or for both of them after their wedding.

When planning a party, it behooves the groom's parents to remember that a shower hosted by a mother of either family is *taboo*.

If the groom's parents live nearby, or even if they don't, they will be invited to showers for the bride or the bride and groom. They should TAKE A GIFT IF THEY ATTEND, and if not, they should try to send a shower gift in care of the hostess.

♦ FINANCIAL OBLIGATIONS: Traditionally, the bride's family paid for the entire wedding and keyed it to their own finances. In the past, if the groom's parents were more affluent, they occasionally assisted by assuming, or contributing to, a portion of the expenses, such as the bar, flowers or limousines. They sometimes offered to pay for wedding announcements they wanted if the bride's family chose not to send any. This help was given behind the scenes, with a private understanding between both sets of parents. These days one may find both families openly sharing expenses—following the custom of some foreign countries—and indeed in many cases the bride and groom themselves will assume all the expenses.

When both families share expenses, the names of both sets of parents should appear on the invitations:

Mr. and Mrs. Bride's Parents
Mr. and Mrs. Groom's Parents
request the honour of your presence
at the marriage of
Jennifer (plus last name)
to
Mr. Groom's full name . . . etc.

If the groom is still a student, THE GROOM'S PARENTS MAY WANT TO ASSIST HIM WITH SOME OF HIS RESPONSIBILITIES, if they are able.

Traditionally, the parents of the groom HOST A DINNER FOLLOWING OR PRECEDING THE WEDDING REHEARSAL. *(See pages 156 to 161.)*

The following are additional suggestions for giving from the groom's family:

- An ENGAGEMENT PRESENT FOR THE ENGAGED COUPLE, perhaps silver, a family heirloom, a more extensive honeymoon trip than the groom can afford, furniture for their new home or a check.

- A PERSONAL GIFT FOR THE BRIDE—perhaps a piece of jewelry.

- In rare situations the groom's parents may offer to

GIVE THE WEDDING. This would be a case where for some reason the bride's parents are unable to do it; perhaps both her parents are deceased and there are no other relatives to take over, or her parents may live in a foreign country.

If the groom's parents host the wedding, the invitations should be worded as follows:

> *Mr. and Mrs. Groom's Parents' Name*
> *request the honour of your presence*
> *at the marriage of*
> *Miss (or Ms.) Bride's Name*
> *to their son*
> *Mr. Groom's Name . . . etc.*

This is the correct form for a church wedding; a home wedding invitation would read "request the pleasure of your company."

- GENERAL PLANS: These plans are directed to the traditional wedding. *Cooperation is the keynote.* The groom's family should cooperate with all the bride's plans and not attempt to make any decisions on their own. Here are a few examples:

  * Keep *their guest list to the number of places allotted them* by the bride's parents. The bride's parents may be limited by space or budget.

  * They should *submit their guest list on or ahead of schedule;* this is important!

* They should spare the bride the tedious task of *organizing their guest list*. The list should be done on a computer (at least typewritten), or on 3″ × 5″ cards, and it should include each guest's full name (no initials), address and zip code:

> *Carter, Mr. and Mrs. John Alfred*
> *810 Fifth Avenue*
> *San Francisco, California 94406*

The same procedure is used for the announcement list, provided announcements are to be ordered.

* The groom's family may offer to *help address invitations,* but should not be offended if the bride and her mother find it less confusing to do it themselves, or to hire a calligrapher.

♦ WHAT TO WEAR: The bride's mother will select her outfit first, then expect the mother of the groom to coordinate her color and style. *(See pages 102 to 103.)*

The groom's father should dress in the same style of suit as the men in the wedding party—provided their outfits are traditional.

♦ IN CHURCH: This is the proud moment! Shortly before the processional starts, the grandparents will be seated. Then the head usher will escort the groom's mother to the first pew on the right-hand side. The groom's father will follow a step or two behind and take the aisle seat. If the groom's parents have another son in the wedding party, other than the best man, they may ask that *he* accompany them.

The bride's mother is always the last person to be seated before the ceremony begins.

If the groom's parents have relatives attending the wedding, they should be certain that pews are reserved for them and that they identify themselves to the ushers. *(See pages 161 to 162.)*

The groom's parents should leave the church for the reception as soon as possible after the recessional (at some weddings they may be detained a short time for photographs). If there is to be a receiving line at the reception, it cannot start until they have taken their place in it.

♦ THE RECEIVING LINE, AND AFTER: Now the solemnities are over and it is almost time to relax. The parents of the groom have one last duty, and that is to stand in the receiving line (if there is one) and do their part to keep it moving smoothly. They should not hold up the line by chatting at length with their own friends, but should introduce them promptly to the next person in line. When the line disbands, they will be free to visit.

The mothers *always* stand in the receiving line, and the fathers may or may not do so. The bride makes this decision. *(See pages 124 to 126.)*

Mothers sometimes keep their gloves on, but if

the bride's mother removes hers, the groom's mother should also. Gloves will not be worn at a home wedding.

When it is time for the bride and groom to leave on their honeymoon, one of their attendants will take the groom's parents to them for a quick hug and a kiss.

And finally—a toast to them and their enduring future happiness.

A Little Paperwork

Whether you do it by the old-fashioned but reliable card file method or by computer, for which there are several programs readily available, it is imperative that you have all of the following information **organized** and available at your fingertips.

WEDDING PARTY LIST

Make a complete alphabetical file of your wedding party, with names, addresses including e-mail, telephone numbers including cell phones and faxes. Duplicate lists should be available for parents, the wedding party and friends who will want to include them in pre-wedding parties.

THE GUEST LIST

When making your guest list, keep in mind that you should expect that approximately three-fourths of those you invite will attend. This will determine the number of guests you can safely invite.

The guest list will start with your own family and friends and those of your father and mother, who will want to include a few close personal and business friends and their spouses. The groom and his parents will also add their lists. In addition to these, if you are a member of the church in which your wedding is to be held, or if your parents or the groom's parents know the officiating clergyman, it is traditional to invite him and his wife to the reception. They are not expected to send a gift. The church wedding coordinator or secretary, if you are acquainted with her, will also appreciate an invitation to the reception.

Do not complete your wedding guest list in haste. At first thought you might feel that if you invite one person from your book club, you must invite them all. Take the time to think it over and invite only those who are special to you in some way. Each guest on your list should be personally selected.

Others to consider when you are making your guest list are:

- ◆ THE GROOM'S PARENTS. Although they are well aware of the wedding date, be sure to mail them an invitation. They will want to keep it.

- ◆ PARENTS, BROTHERS AND SISTERS OF THE MEMBERS OF YOUR WEDDING PARTY.

- ◆ SEPARATE INVITATIONS FOR ANY PERSON EIGHTEEN YEARS OR OLDER. An exception to this is that you may send joint invitations to two or more brothers or sisters living at the same address.

◆ Close friends living at a great distance consider it a compliment to receive an invitation. However, if you feel that an invitation seems to call for a gift, you may prefer to send ANNOUNCEMENTS to less intimate friends. This is your decision.

◆ If you wish single guests to bring a DATE OR ESCORT, write on the inner envelope beneath the name, "Please bring an escort (or date)," or you may enclose a note. You might prefer to ask for the name and address and mail a separate invitation—especially to a friend's fiancé. This is one reason extra invitations will come in handy.

◆ If a couple is LIVING TOGETHER AS A "COUPLE" and not merely roommates, address the invitation to the one with whom you are best acquainted and include both names on the inner envelope (as well as on your guest list). If you are equally acquainted with each, write both names on the outer and on the inner envelopes.

Discuss with the groom's family the number of guests you can accommodate. If they live in the same area, they are entitled to half the guests, if they so desire. Some couples with a large coterie of friends divide the invitation numbers with ¼ of the guests allotted for each set of parents and ½ for the bride and groom. Others do ⅓, ⅓ and ⅓. Work this out according to your own situation, but remember to be gracious and generous to the groom's family. If they live far removed, they probably will not need as many invitations. You will need their list early, so give them a final cut-off date.

Record prospective guests on your list as follows:

> Carter, Mr. and Mrs. John Alfred
> 810 Fifth Avenue
> San Francisco, California 94406

The names on the guest list should be filed alphabetically. Go over and over these names, and *think* as you go. You will remember that Mr. and Mrs. Carter have a daughter who is eighteen. She should receive a separate invitation (do not economize on this), so list her name and address separately. The bridesmaids may have brothers and sisters and parents to be invited individually (never put "and Family" on an invitation), and their names will go into the correct place on your list. You may want to devise a code to distinguish between your list and the groom's list. Other codes might be "R" for "reception," "A" for "announcement only" or whatever suits your individual plan.

Please remember that it is NOT necessary to invite everyone to the ceremony who comes to the reception. Many brides (and grooms) prefer a smaller, more intimate ceremony where they are not so much "on show." This may be followed by a large and festive wedding reception. A bride and groom should never feel obliged to invite all of their guests to the ceremony if they are uncomfortable doing so.

The purpose of a wedding announcement is informational only, and it is usually sent to inform people from out of town. Recipients of wedding announcements are not expected to send wedding gifts.

You will need to have an alphabetical master list to record responses to the wedding invitations. Keep this in a convenient place near where you open your mail. As the responses arrive, cross off the names of those who regret, and note the *number* of those who accept. This method will make it easy to arrive at a final total. Be careful and accurate! This will save last-minute embarrassments and make it easy to give a true count to the caterer at zero hour.

Duplicate the guest list for the groom's parents. They will appreciate the chance to familiarize themselves with the names of those they don't already know, so they will feel at ease at the reception.

The guest list may also be used when you are asked for a list of friends to invite to a party in your honor. Unless there are unusual circumstances, guests should not be invited to wedding showers or parties unless they are invited to the wedding.

MAKING A CALENDAR

How you decide to do this is up to you, but it is important for you to have a reminder system of some sort. It will help with your peace of mind as activities intensify and your excitement begins to build. A carefully constructed calendar means you won't have to worry about any responsibility until the day it appears.

Computer programs work well, or you can purchase a regular paper calendar. Write the item that needs to be done under the day it needs to be accomplished and then FORGET about it until that day. Be sure to place the calendar in a place that you see each day, and don't let yourself procrastinate! If you put off too many "to do's," your wedding will not be as serene as you hoped, and neither will you.

KEEPING TRACK OF YOUR WEDDING GIFTS

It is time to prepare for the wedding gifts that will begin to arrive very quickly.

Purchase a notebook (bridal shops will carry those specifically made for wedding gifts) in which to register wedding gifts as they arrive. When a gift arrives, list it by number in your gift register and tape a duplicate number to the gift. Be sure to record the name of the store in the register. This will be a help in checking errors and is indispensable if gifts have to be returned. (Exchanges are permissible providing you use discretion.) It is helpful to save the boxes of gifts you know will have to be exchanged.

When you check your guest list for the address of the donor to whom you are writing a thank-you letter, keep a record of the date you mailed your thank-you note. This, along with your wedding gift register, will give you a quick reference and will help you meet many a diplomatic crisis. A quick check will instantly remind you of the treasure Great-Aunt Agatha sent and when you acknowledged it.

If you are going on an extended honeymoon trip, or moving to another city, it is wise to list which gifts are to be stored, exchanged or shipped. Make these notes in your gift register. If you are to be away from home for a lengthy time, you will need someone to send you a list of gifts as they arrive so you can keep up with your thank-you notes during this period.

Keep the groom's family updated with copies of the gift list so they will know what their friends have sent. Brides have discovered that if everyone uses the same source of reference, it promotes understanding and co-operation, and avoids diverse opinions and dissension "within the ranks."

ANNOUNCING YOUR ENGAGEMENT IN THE PRESS

Most large city newspapers don't carry announcements anymore, although many smaller local newspapers do. You should contact the papers in which you are interested, to inquire about each one's policy. Ask if they accept photographs and obtain information about timing for later wedding submissions.

One news release will suffice provided you and your fiancé are from the same city. If he and his parents live or have connections elsewhere, send those papers the item with a date "to be released . . ."

Traditionally your parents make the announcement. An engagement announcement starts with words to this effect:

"Mr. and Mrs. Douglas Andrew Blake of Pasadena, California, announce the engagement of their daughter, Sharon Anne, to Mr. Jeffrey Paul Fowler, Jr., the son of Mr. and Mrs. Jeffrey Paul Fowler of Stamford, Connecticut. A December wedding is planned in Pasadena . . ."

The announcement continues with a brief resume about the couple's schooling, occupations, wedding date and future residence. A smaller hometown paper might like to include the names of the grandparents of longtime residents.

You may compose your own announcement, or request an engagement form (and a wedding form to use later). The forms makes it easier to conform to each paper's individual style. Some newspapers will accept only announcements completed on their own forms.

If one of the parents is no longer living, refer to him or her as "the late" Mr. or Mrs. in the body of the article. For example, "Mrs. Douglas Andrew Blake announces the engagement of her daughter, Sharon Anne, to . . ." etc. Then further into the release ". . . She is also the daughter of the late Mr. . . ."

PLANNING FOR
OUT-OF-TOWN GUESTS

Very common today is the "destination wedding," or a wedding that includes several days of activities for out-of-town guests. Did you know that Labor Day weekend has replaced the month of June as the most popular time to get married?

With this in mind, those who choose to have a wedding of this sort need to let their out-of-town friends know well in advance—six to eight months is none too soon!—so that guests may make necessary travel plans and book accommodations. This is done with a "save the date" card, information letter or personally designed brochure. Some couples like to design their own websites to keep everyone advised of up-to-date happenings.

The save-the-date card may be as informal as you wish with your own personal touches, but the following information should be included:

- The DATE, TIME AND LOCATION of the wedding.

- A TENTATIVE SCHEDULE FOR THE WEEKEND, with blocks of time indicated for activities already planned as well as for those that will be determined more specifically at a later date. (Try to include long-distance travelers in at least one group activity each day, be it a hike, baseball game, casual picnic, tennis tournament, luncheon or cocktail party. These guests have made an effort to come thousands of miles for your special day, and they should not be ignored. Specific invitations and/or schedules for these events may be mailed at a later date.)

- RECOMMENDED ACCOMMODATIONS at different price levels with information about group discounts, if any. Guests should be advised to make reservations as soon as possible.

- CAR RENTAL INFORMATION.

- CHILD CARE PROVISIONS, if any. This is "beyond the call of duty," but if you care to take on this responsibility, now is the time to inform your guests.

- A MAP WITH DIRECTIONS to the wedding, to the rehearsal and to any other locations that are key to the weekend.

- A list of a few of the BEST RESTAURANTS AND LOCAL HIGH SPOTS. If you like, you may designate one or two of these as "wedding central," or places where guests may meet each other and socialize.

- Expected LOCAL TEMPERATURES AND CLOTHING SUGGESTIONS.

- A WARM AND ENTHUSIASTIC NOTE from you and your fiancé, personally signed.

It is your responsibility to plan housing arrangements for out-of-town members of the wedding party. If friends offer to house your guests, accept gratefully.

A frequent alternative to this is to reserve rooms for ALL your out-of-town guests at the same hotel or motel, to simplify transportation. Often hotels/motels will give block discount rates for a large group. If possible, it is advisable to give a choice of places to stay at different rate levels.

HOUSEGUESTS

Before you are tempted to house even your best friend at your own home, consider the hazards of houseguests. The best-meaning and most beloved relatives and friends can be very wearing when you are busy and need to conserve your energy. Guests expect to be entertained, they are usually starving and they might drain all the hot water in the house at a critical moment—just when the bride intended to shampoo her hair.

After you have considered these hazards and alternatives, does your hospitable nature still overrule your practical sense of caution? If so, consider a compromise. Your parents might invite your guests to stay for a few days of happy reminiscing *after* the wedding! If you are still feeling hospitable, read on for suggestions and reminders to help make your preparations easier and your houseguests more comfortable.

Getting ready for houseguests, whether before or

after the wedding, will mean preparations and perhaps some reorganizing, but the anticipation of seeing relatives or close friends keeps it all from becoming a chore. No two homes have identical facilities or are run the same, but everyone can consider the following:

- Remember JET LAG. Flying from the West Coast to the East Coast presents little problem the first day. However, don't schedule a dinner party for westbound travelers the first evening unless they arrive early enough to take a rest. By the dinner hour, their built-in clocks will scream "bedtime." Transoceanic flights create even more severe time lags.

- INVITE GUESTS FOR A SPECIFIED LENGTH OF TIME. Planning will be easier if you know exactly how long guests will stay.

- Give houseguests both PRIVACY AND FREEDOM to do what they want—rest, read, walk or sit in the sun. Don't schedule every moment, although it is your town and you know what it has to offer. Make suggestions and give them a city guide marked with "don't miss" signs.

- Before retiring, settle PLANS FOR THE MORNING— breakfast together or each on his own (with a kitchen-orientation tour.) No coffee-holic should have to wait. Prepare the coffeepot before bed and set it to start in plenty of time the next morning.

- If you are used to running your home informally,

everyone will be more comfortable if you DON'T STRAIN TO CHANGE YOUR STYLE.

+ Give the GUEST QUARTERS an extremely critical eye check; better yet, spend a night there yourself. Be sure to check:

  * Reading and makeup lights

  * Assorted short reading matter

  * Pen, pencil, notepaper

  * Blankets

  * Extra pillows

  * Clothes hangers for dresses, skirts and trousers

  * Bathroom supplies: all the essentials, plus conveniences such as scissors, cleansing tissues, bath oil, lotions, hair spray, nail file, hair dryer

+ MAKE THE GUESTROOM INVITING with a bouquet of flowers or a plant or a bowl of fruit and bottles or a vacuum jug of fresh drinking water.

+ Feel free to KEEP YOUR OWN IMPORTANT APPOINTMENTS or to do household errands. Your guests will understand.

+ If your guests have other friends who live in the area, assure them they are free to MAKE ENGAGEMENTS ON THEIR OWN.

+ Let guests MAKE THEIR OWN BEDS (unless you run a hotel-style establishment).

- If you have HIRED HELP in the house, pay them a bonus for their extra efforts. (In the past, guests might have followed the custom of leaving a tip or sending a personal gift to longtime regular help. As household help is less prevalent these days, these niceties are seldom seen, but should your guests ask about leaving a tip, tell them it has been taken care of.)

- Do not spend HOURS IN THE KITCHEN when you have houseguests! Cook meals ahead for the freezer or bring home some of the wonderful freshly prepared take-out food that is so readily available. Eating out is definitely an option. Be sensitive to special diets your guests may follow.

- Give your guests TRANSPORTATION ASSISTANCE on the wedding day, especially if they are unfamiliar with the area. Ask friends to pick them up, lend them your car or engage a driver. If they have their own car, give them a map, estimated travel time and plenty of leeway in case they aren't expert "pathfinders."

Now here is your surprise reward in return for your hospitality. Nothing could be more priceless in the last few days before the wedding than an extra pair of hands, legs, ears, eyes and one sane brain. Count on one of your houseguests to be a buffer to answer the phone and doorbells, accept deliveries, post gift numbers in the register, press out a wrinkle and generally relieve and shield you by making minor decisions.

Getting into It

Things are heating up, and there are some fun topics discussed in this chapter. Roll up your sleeves and dig in.

PLANNING FOR A HOME WEDDING

If the reception is to be held in your home, begin now to plan for the garden, house décor and cleaning of the house before the reception. Refer to home and garden weddings. *(See pages 178 to 192.)*

YOUR WEDDING GOWN AND VEIL

You will find that selecting a wedding gown is one of the most exciting aspects of wedding planning—and, understandably, a happy tearjerker for your mother if she shops with you.

Now that tradition is undeniably back in high favor, wedding gowns are more beautiful than ever—all so lovely that it is difficult to choose just a single one.

Along with the return to tradition, it naturally follows that many brides love the sentiment of wearing the gowns worn by their mothers, aunts or sisters. If the gown was properly "heirloomed" or preserved (an after-the-wedding duty), you already have a big advantage; however, if it has slightly yellowed, call it "ivory." You may also find services that specialize in restoring wedding gowns, if yours needs it. It is amazing what experts can do, so don't be discouraged from wearing a damaged heirloom wedding gown until you have checked with them.

Skilled designers have both the vision and expertise to transform a size six gown into a size ten, and then challenge you to find the alteration points. A lace veil previously worn by another might not be becoming in its original state, but it, too, can be skillfully redesigned to flatter and delight you.

The following are some points to consider as you are making your selection:

- Allow an absolute MINIMUM OF SIX MONTHS if your gown has to be ordered, then fitted.

- Gowns range in price from moderate to enormous. Before you shop, decide HOW MUCH YOU CAN COMFORTABLY SPEND.

- Choose a wedding gown that is APPROPRIATE for

the time of day, and consistent with the formality or informality of your overall plan:

* Formal daytime or evening: long gown, short or long train, long, fingertip or short veil.

* Summer garden: lighter-weight fabric without a train. (Frequently gowns are made so that the train can be removed before the reception.)

* Informal morning: suit, or street-length dress with or without a jacket, no veil, hat optional.

* Informal evening: long or short cocktail dress.

♦ As for GLOVES, if your gown has long sleeves, there is no need for them. With a short-sleeved, sleeveless or strapless dress, consider:

* Short gloves that are slightly large so that you can slip off the left glove and give it to the maid of honor to hold.

* Fingerless mitts.

* Long white gloves that you will not remove. Either roll back to the wrist, or have the store rip the seams of the ring finger.

* You will wear your engagement ring on your right hand the day of the wedding so the wedding ring can properly be placed first on your finger.

* Gloves are inappropriate at a small home wedding.

- At a SMALL HOME WEDDING a short or long dress, in white or a soft color, with or without a short veil, is suitable. If the wedding is limited to family and a few close friends, you may prefer to be married in your going-away suit or dress without a veil.

- Buy the WEDDING SHOES AND UNDERTHINGS before the fitting.

- After you've had your gown fitted, don't go impulsively on a CRASH DIET. You might discover too late that although you shrank, your gown didn't. Conversely, it would be even worse to *gain* weight after your fitting!

- If your BUDGET won't stretch as far as you would like, investigate other alternatives:

  * Ready-to-wear gowns.

  * End-of-season sales.

  * If you can step into a sample model, occasionally you can buy the sample for less than the same style if you ordered it.

  * Discount outlets.

  * Rented gowns at less than half their original retail cost.

  * Borrowing from a friend, sister or cousin.

  * Some rental shops buy only from the bridal gown manufacturers. Others will buy once-used

gowns to add to their rental inventory. This option will require diligent research on your part.
Happy Hunting!

YOUR WEDDING SHOES

Purchase your wedding shoes before the final fitting of your wedding dress, and wear them around the house a bit to break them in. You should be comfortable in them and used to the height of the heel so that you won't wobble going down the aisle. If they are silk, have them treated with a stain-resistant spray.

DRESSING YOUR BRIDESMAIDS

When the time comes to select bridesmaids' dresses and headpieces, it is better not to shop en masse, because if you have six bridesmaids, you are likely to have six different opinions. Discuss with them a satisfactory price range; customarily they pay for their own outfits.

Remember that a popular girl's closet might already be filled with dressy, unwearable gowns from previous bridesmaid stints. Try to find dresses they "can't wait to wear again," or can have remodeled later. Selecting dresses in a color or style to fit assorted sizes, shapes, coloring and tastes is not an easy assignment, but with patient effort, you can accomplish wonders.

In addition to choosing a color that is becoming to

your attendants, visualize it in the church and reception settings. For example, shell pink might look enchanting in a light and airy church, while stronger jewel tones would complement cathedral architecture. If you are in doubt, take a color sample and judge it in the settings where it will be worn.

If the bridesmaids are geographically scattered, have their dresses delivered to them in time to have any needed alterations. If you know a good, reliable and prompt seamstress in the town where the wedding is taking place, you can live a little more dangerously and have final alterations done after the bridesmaids arrive. In this case, however, the seamstress should already have the dresses made to order to the bridesmaids' predetermined measurements. In this way only minor alterations should remain.

Bridesmaids customarily pay for their own outfits. Here are two possible budget stretchers for them: the dresses can be made to your specifications at home, or by a dressmaker, or you can shop for rental bridesmaid dresses. It is even more difficult to find rentals for bridesmaids than for brides, but perhaps your perseverance will be rewarded. Also, don't rule out shopping for dresses "off the rack" at a department store. They often have a large selection and range of sizes.

Here is one further thought about the cost of bridesmaids' gowns. If the entire wedding is lavish, and the selected dresses wildly expensive, the bride's parents may pay for them—while rationalizing that the gowns are part of the "wedding décor." A fantasy solution!

In your records, keep track of the store and the salesperson from whom you have purchased the dresses. Also record your bridesmaids' dress measurements as a double check for the store.

As of this writing, there are brides who depart from the tradition of having the bridesmaids all dressed *exactly* the same, that is, with matching jewelry, makeup, gloves, pantyhose and shoes. It is lovely to match everything if you can, but some of today's young women want a little more freedom in what they wear. You'll be pretty safe if you tell your attendants to wear a single strand of pearls (the difference in sizes will not be too evident), but I would not tell them to wear whatever jewelry they choose. The same holds for shoes, i.e., they should all be the same color, but a slight variation in style will not make that much difference. I recently heard of a bride who let her bridesmaids wear cocktail dresses of their own choice. You may also choose the fabric and color for the bridesmaids' dresses, and allow your attendants to wear it in different styles. Whatever your preference is, by all means go for it, but be aware that in some cases this freedom might not make the magical, well-thought-out statement you deserve on your wedding day.

After you have made your selection, keep in mind the following specifics:

- If you wish to have HEADPIECES for your attendants, decide on them now. They may be hats, ribbons or fresh flower adornments from the florist.

- If you have invited a JUNIOR BRIDESMAID or flower girl, select a harmonizing dress suitable for her age.

- If you can, ask the fitter to CORRELATE THE LENGTHS of the bridesmaids' dresses; it will look better in the church and in photographs.

- If you wish to COORDINATE YOUR ATTENDANTS' MAKEUP, take a dress fabric sample with you when you purchase lipstick and nail polish.

- If all bridesmaids are to wear the SAME SHOES, be sure to have them all dyed in the same dye lot.

- Again, for the WELL-COORDINATED LOOK, select the proper shade of pantyhose to go with your dresses and buy a pair for each bridesmaid in her size, plus a few extra in case of an emergency.

- In terms of JEWELRY, it is preferable that bridesmaids not wear watches or bracelets. Simple earrings and a delicate necklace are enough.

DRESSING THE MOTHERS

The mother of the bride is the first to select her dress, and it should complement the bridesmaids' dresses in color and style.

When the mother of the bride has selected her outfit, she can describe it to the groom's mother: length of dress, length of sleeves, color and degree of formality. To create a harmonious picture in photographs and the receiving line, colors and styles should be coordinated. It is customary for the bride or her mother to suggest a selection of colors from which the groom's mother may choose. As a rule, black dresses are not suitable for this happy occasion, although all-black weddings, always black tie and in the evening, are seen occasionally.

At a home wedding, the mothers do not wear hats or gloves. If the home wedding is limited to family and close friends, the mothers may wear something they already have that is becoming and suitable for the time of day.

MEN'S ATTIRE

What the men wear is established by the pattern of the wedding—its setting, time of day, degree of formality, the bride's gown and season of the year. Customs vary in different parts of the country for no discernible reason, so this book can only state what is reasonably proper. Here are the general categories and what they entail:

- FORMAL DAYTIME: Oxford gray cutaway coat, striped gray or black trousers, lighter gray waistcoat, a starched wing collar with an ascot or a starched regular collar with a four-in-hand tie, gray doeskin gloves (to be removed at the reception), plain-toed black shoes with black socks, pearl or black studs, pearl or gold cuff links.

- SEMIFORMAL DAYTIME: Short Oxford gray director's coat, double-breasted gray waistcoat, four-in-hand tie, gray doeskin gloves (to be removed at the reception), plain black shoes with black socks, pearl or gold jewelry.

- INFORMAL DAYTIME: Oxford gray or dark blue suit, white shirt, four-in-hand tie, black shoes and socks, black or gold jewelry.

- SUMMER INFORMAL: (in the country or suburbs) Navy blue blazer with gray or white flannel trousers or a lightweight summer suit, four-in-hand tie.

- FORMAL EVENING: Tailcoat, white piqué waistcoat, stiff-bosomed shirt with starched wing collar and white bow tie, black dress pumps with black socks, white kid gloves, pearl jewelry.

- SEMIFORMAL EVENING: (after 6 P.M.) Black or midnight blue dinner jacket, black or midnight blue vest or cummerbund and matching bow tie, white dress shirt, black plain-toed shoes or dress pumps with black socks, black or gold jewelry.

- SUMMER SEMIFORMAL: The same as "semiformal evening," substituting a white dinner jacket, if that is an acceptable style in your locale.

- INFORMAL EVENING: Dark business suit, plain white shirt, four-in-hand tie, black shoes and socks.

Here is some general information on men's wedding attire:

- The groom, best man, ushers and both fathers wear the same type of suit and accessories. If the fathers choose not to do this, then they should not stand in the receiving line.

♦ All the ushers' ascots or ties should be alike, but they should be different from the ones worn by the groom and the best man.

♦ All the ushers should wear the same variety of boutonnieres, such as white carnations, while the groom and best man may wear lily-of-the-valley boutonnieres pinned to their left lapels.

♦ No tuxedos should ever be worn before six o'clock in the evening!

♦ PLAIN white shirts are best.

WEDDING TRANSPORTATION

This can be difficult! It is important to dot your i's and cross your t's in this regard, as there is nothing worse than a disgruntled family member or member of the bridal party who has been left out of the loop in terms of getting from here to there. You must be careful not only to organize their transportation, but also *to let them know the plan and with whom they are riding*.

Hire a well-documented and responsible limousine service or arrange with friends to take the wedding party to the church and from the church to the reception. This may mean multiple pickups at different places, depending on where people are dressing, or where the photos are being taken if they are done before the ceremony. Inform each member of the bridal party with whom he/she is riding so that they may be together at the time of pickup. The drivers should be informed of whom they are driving, i.e., bride and father, parents, grandparents, etc., where they are to be picked up and where they are to be taken.

If you hire limousines, determine the color you want (white or black is preferable) ahead of time, if you have a preference, and the size. Arrange for payment either before or after the wedding day. Record the name and phone number of the service you use. If you use friends, make a note of their names and numbers, too.

Here are a few notes on transportation:

- The BRIDE AND HER FATHER, traditionally, have their own limousine (car) to take them to the church.

- The BRIDESMAIDS travel to the church in limousine(s) or car(s). They may go from the church to the reception in limousines/cars, or with the ushers if the USHERS PROMISE TO ARRIVE PROMPTLY.

- The BRIDE'S MOTHER may ride with the bridesmaids to the church and with the father of the bride to the reception.

- The PARENTS OF THE GROOM should have a driver so that they may arrive at the reception promptly, especially if there is to be a receiving line.

- Provisions also need to be made for the GRANDPAR-

ENTS and the CHILDREN in the wedding party. If the children go with a driver, their parents should be invited to do so, too. (Their parents may also drive them.)

- The following information should be given to all DRIVERS, car or limousine:

  * Information on where to pick up each passenger.

  * Exact times for pickups.

  * Estimated time to travel destination. (Allow a little latitude when estimating the timing.)

  * A clearly designated map.

STATIONERY, MONOGRAMS AND SIGNING YOUR NEW NAME

If you want to order monogrammed stationery for your thank-you letters, you must use your own initials until you are married, so don't overbuy unless you are retaining your maiden name.

Here is a list of basics that will help you choose the letter papers that suit *your* lifestyle.

- EVERYDAY PAPER for household or business-type letters—even chatty letters to longtime friends. It is convenient to have this printed with your married name and address on single sheets.

- Engraved fold-over INFORMALS or single French cards are useful for invitations, responses and short thank-yous and to enclose with gifts. "Mr. and Mrs." and "Mrs." only are made from the same die (a piece of engraved metal used to imprint your monogram, initial or name on your stationery). If your address is relatively permanent, it may also be engraved on the stationery. Your stationery may also be thermographed, a much less expensive but nevertheless attractive process. Only the experts will be able to tell the difference.

- A box of PERFECTLY PLAIN, best quality white or off-white paper for formal responses and letters of condolence.

- GOOD-QUALITY NOTE PAPER or correspondence cards for notes and invitations. Monogram if you wish, or postpone ordering a die. As time goes on, both your needs and taste could change. In the meantime, handsome bordered papers in interesting color combinations are available.

- Printed MEMOS OR POSTCARDS are handy for brief notes.

- If you use your MAIDEN NAME PROFESSIONALLY, order business stationery to fit your needs.

If you are monogramming your stationery, the first initial of your husband's surname is the largest or accentuated initial of the monogram, usually centered, and flanked by the first initial of your first name on the left, and the initial of your maiden name on the right. If you retain your maiden name, stationery may be engraved or processed with both your names—yours on the first line, his on the second. For engraved calling cards and informals, use "Mr. and Mrs." and full name including the middle name. *No initials.*

When monogramming silver, use the single initial of your husband's surname, or follow the styles for stationery. Silver may be engraved on the front or back of the handle tips. Silver is often passed down from one generation to another. If it is already monogrammed with initials other than your own, use it with pride.

Towels and bed linens are monogrammed in the same manner as stationery.

For fun and informality, such as on bar glasses, you can combine your and your husband's first-name initials.

Signing Your Name After You Are Married

- If you TAKE YOUR HUSBAND'S NAME, you will sign your name on checks and legal papers as given name, maiden name or initial and husband's name, i.e., Barbara Townsend Long.

- In LETTERS TO CLOSE FRIENDS, you will always be Barbara.

- To THOSE WHO WILL RECOGNIZE YOUR NEW NAME, you will sign Barbara Long. If they might need a clue, sign Barbara Townsend Long.

- For committee-type or BUSINESS LETTERS, sign Barbara Townsend Long. Under your signature you may write in parentheses (Mrs. Kenneth Long).

- Some couples agree to HYPHENATE THEIR SUR-NAMES, such as Mr. and Mrs. Kenneth Townsend-Long. Infrequently, they reverse their last names. In this example it would be Mr. and Mrs. Kenneth Long-Townsend.

- If you DO NOT ASSUME YOUR HUSBAND'S NAME, clarify by using a printed letterhead with your name alone and, for joint letters, your name on one line and his on the line below.

- Did you know that legally you may use TWO OR MORE NAMES? You may, therefore, keep properties and selected accounts in your present name, while using your married name socially and for joint as-sets. If a time occurs when you are uncertain about which name to sign, you may sign both names this way: One name/aka/other name. (The initials "aka" stand for "also known as.")

- DO NOT SIGN LETTERS JOINTLY as Kenneth and Barbara, except for gift and greeting cards. Instead, mention your husband in the body of the letter.

REGISTERING FOR WEDDING GIFTS

You and the groom should select and register for your silver, china, crystal and other household items. Often the groom is not as domestically oriented as his bride-to-be, so to save confusion you might want to do some preliminary looking, then go together to make final decisions. Make a list of all the stores at which you are registered. Friends will often ask where you are registered, bless their hearts. Several of the larger stores are on-line with their registries—a tremendous convenience, especially for out-of-town friends.

Selecting your very own china, crystal, silver, furniture and accessories is a joyous and exciting time. Here is your chance to create your home in the taste and style you want.

Even if you know your lifestyle will be modest at first, try to project your thinking to envision a later time in your lives when you will entertain with more than stainless steel and wooden salad bowls. If you have to store these more elegant possessions in the family's attic for a while, it will be a double treat when you finally retrieve and use them.

♦ SILVER: Silver is so expensive that you would be thrilled to acquire one piece at a time. In deference to your friends, ask the store personnel to quote the cost of individual pieces, not complete place settings. Today many couples choose to register for stainless flatware. Remember, however, that sterling is meant to be used daily and will last for generations. With use, silver attains a beautiful mellow look.

♦ CRYSTAL: No matter how costly, crystal chips and breaks. Ask any long-married person about her crystal inventory. She will probably report something like "seven goblets, nine wineglasses, a dozen sherbets" (because the sherbets are used less often). Aim for sixteen or eighteen instead of the usual dozen of each kind, and don't burden yourselves with the most expensive crystal in the world. Your family might give you the pieces you did not receive for future special occasions.

- CHINA: If you choose an expensive make of china, as with your silverware, again ask the store to quote prices of individual pieces instead of place settings. You might not even want complete matching place settings. Many people of style believe their dinner tables are more interesting if they use a different pattern for each course as long as the feeling is compatible—not delicate china and bold pottery at the same meal.

- EVERYDAY DISHES: Register your everyday dishes, too. Being less costly than your good china, the price range will please some givers. Try to select a pattern you won't tire of with constant use.

- GOURMET HOMEWARES AND OTHER REGISTRIES: Gourmet specialty shops stock excitingly handsome and utilitarian homewares. Brides love to register their needs and desires at such a shop. Besides cookware, you will be tempted to register everything else you see. If you register at such a shop, be sure to tell friends who ask. The guys are getting into the act as well, and couples will sometimes register at a hard-

ware or sportsgear store. Be sure to inform your
friends!

If you make a point of registering your desires in a
wide price range, it will indicate that you would be as
delighted to receive an inexpensive bud vase or pepper
mill as you would a sterling silver platter.

Register your gifts in more than one store. If you
live in the suburbs but are inviting friends from the city
to your wedding, register in both places. If you register
the same patterns or duplicate objects in more than one
store, update the listings periodically. Notify the other
stores when the desired quantity has been reached.

In some areas you will find discount houses where
china, crystal and silver patterns may be purchased at
sizable discounts. When you register in a place such as
this, be careful and be sure to read the fine print.
Usually these stores require a minimum quantity to be
purchased; if you do not reach that number by a certain date, you will be charged for the difference.

If no one will be at home to receive your gifts when
they are delivered, make special arrangements with the
stores to deliver only on certain days or to hold the
gifts until you notify them.

YOUR TROUSSEAU

The word "trousseau" might sound old-fashioned or
archaic, like "dowry." Dictionaries, however, offer no
synonym. "Trousseau" is defined as the bride's posses-

sions, particularly clothes and linens. So *whatever* clothes and linens—old or new—you bring to your marriage become a part of your trousseau. In usage today, buying a trousseau means replenishing and augmenting.

Parents love to help replenish and augment to whatever degree they can afford, and to share their daughter's thrill of acquiring her "trousseau." Selecting is a highly individual and personal matter, but a few suggestions follow:

◆ It will be a joy to start your married life with an assortment of pretty, new, feminine and ROMANTIC LINGERIE.

◆ It used to be considered essential to send a bride off with ENOUGH CLOTHING to last at least a year, until her young husband could provide for her. Today's bride prefers the option of adding when the seasons, styles and needs change. Some generous parents allow their daughter a "credit" for an additional outfit or two during the year.

◆ Some marriages will bring about a CHANGE OF RESIDENCE, location or manner of living, so buy accordingly.

◆ Look over the clothes already in your closet to decide what can be renovated to fit your future lifestyle and make a LIST OF WHAT IS REQUIRED to fill out your wardrobe.

◆ A "GOING-AWAY" OUTFIT to wear when leaving the

reception has traditionally been something tailored and suitable for your destination or travel plans. Today most brides will prepare a going-away outfit even though they plan to return for a Sunday morning brunch for out-of-town guests the next day. There are other brides, however, who forgo the going-away outfit completely and prefer to leave the reception in their bridal finery.

◆ Concerning YOUR LINEN AND HOUSEHOLD TROUSSEAU, this is the ideal time, and your opportunity, to review and evaluate your family's style and customs from your growing-up days. Determine those practices with which you are comfortable and admire, and want to maintain, and those styles and standards of your own you want to establish.

Linens will probably come to you as shower or wedding gifts. If you live away from home, you already have some of the basics. Maybe your parents have shared, or will share, some of their expendables with you. From all these sources you have a good start.

Below is a worksheet of items upon which to base your trousseau choices. Add or subtract to suit yourself. This list may also be used when registering for your wedding gifts.

◆ FOR THE DINING ROOM: placemats for breakfast (handsome plastic ones are cheerful and practical), luncheon placemats or cloths and napkins, placemats and napkins for informal and formal dinners, tablecloths for elegant dinners and buffet suppers, with extra napkins (white is practical, as it can be bleached to take out stains).

- COCKTAIL NAPKINS (although most use paper these days).

- PICNIC CLOTHS AND NAPKINS.

- FOR THE BEDROOM: top sheets (three for each bed), fitted bottom sheets (three for each bed), pillow cases (four for each pillow), blankets, comforters or electric blankets, blanket covers, duvets and covers, mattress covers, bedspread and dust ruffle.

- FOR THE BATHROOM: bath towels, hand towels, washcloths, bath mats, guest towels, beach towels.

- FOR THE KITCHEN: dish towels, dishcloths, cleaning cloths, dust cloths.

Should you wish to monogram any of your linens, follow the instructions listed under stationery in this book. *(See pages 107 to 109.)*

ORDERING INVITATIONS AND ANNOUNCEMENTS

As soon as you have decided on the number of guests, order your wedding invitations and announcements. Be sure to allow plenty of time, including the addressing, so that the invitations can be mailed six to eight weeks ahead of the wedding. You will need to order extras, as some will be spoiled in addressing.

If you appreciate the elegance of traditional invitations—which will set the tone of your wedding—go to a reputable, established stationer. The very best stationers with experienced personnel charge no more than other stores that might prove unsatisfactory.

Qualified people can advise you on the proper and current styles of lettering, size and quality of paper, and the correct wording for church and home weddings and announcements. They are prepared to give you information about reception cards, map enclosures when needed and "at home" cards, which are enclosed only in announcements.

You might have a special situation—unusual to you but totally familiar to experienced stationers. Their understanding, good taste and knowledge of etiquette can guide you. Second-time brides will find special information later in this book. *(See pages 206 to 208.)*

A number of examples of conventional wedding invitations are included. Those who admire and respect tradition will be interested to know that, according to very old etiquette books, the wording is still the same. Please note that the year is optional on an invitation, but always included on an announcement.

A TRADITIONAL CHURCH WEDDING INVITATION

Mr. and Mrs. Douglas Andrew Blake
request the honour of your presence
at the marriage of their daughter
Sharon Anne
to
Mr. Jeffrey Paul Fowler, Jr.
on Saturday, the twenty-eighth of December
at four o'clock
Church name
Church address (if needed)

A WEDDING NOT IN A CHURCH

Mr. and Mrs. Douglas Andrew Blake
request the pleasure of your company
etc.

A DIVORCED MOTHER

Mrs. Barbara Guest or Mrs. Townsend Guest
etc.

(This depends on whichever form of your name you customarily use. The latter example—using one's maiden surname combined with the former husband's last name—used to be the established, traditional and only "correct" way, but is now used less often.)

IF THE BRIDE'S MOTHER HAS REMARRIED

Mr. and Mrs. Howard Thomas Whiting
request the honour of your presence
at the marriage of her daughter
Sharon Anne Blake
etc.

IF THE FATHER OF THE BRIDE HAS REMARRIED

Mr. and Mrs. Harold Robert Anderson
request the honour of your presence at
the marriage of his daughter
Emily Marie
etc.

GRANDPARENTS, GODPARENTS OR ANOTHER RELATIVE

Mr. and Mrs. Oliver Justin Henry
request the honour of your presence at
the marriage of their granddaughter
Eleanor James
etc.

ADULT CHILDREN OF A WIDOW OR DIVORCÉE

John Alan Henry
Stephen Martin Henry
Elizabeth Hilary Granger
request
the honour of your presence

at the marriage of their mother
Ann
to
Anthony Gordon Donalson
etc.

A BRIDE AND GROOM ON THEIR OWN—AT A CHURCH

The honour of your presence
is requested at the marriage of
Miss Sharon Anne Blake
to
Mr. Jeffrey Paul Fowler, Jr.
etc.

A BRIDE AND GROOM ON THEIR OWN—
OTHER THAN AT A CHURCH

Miss Sharon Anne Blake
and
Mr. Jeffrey Paul Fowler, Jr.
request the pleasure of your company
at their marriage
etc.

FOR A SMALL CEREMONY WITH A LARGER RECEPTION

Mr. and Mrs. Douglas Andrew Blake
request the pleasure of your company
at a reception
in celebration of the marriage of

Miss Sharon Ann Blake
and
Mr. Jeffrey Paul Fowler, Jr.
on Saturday, the twenty-eighth of December
at six o'clock
The Saint Matthew Hotel
Union Square
San Francisco

In the following invitation, a small ceremony card
would be included for those also invited to the ceremony:

We cordially request the pleasure of your company
at the ceremony
at half after four o'clock
United Cathedral
3660 Adam Boulevard
San Francisco

ANNOUNCEMENTS

These follow the pattern of the invitations:

Mr. and Mrs. Douglas Andrew Blake
have the honour of announcing
the marriage of their daughter
Sharon Anne
to
Mr. Jeffrey Paul Fowler, Jr.
Saturday, the twenty-eighth of December
two thousand and three
Location (city, or city and state).

Please note that the year is always included on an announcement, but is optional on an invitation.

When ordering your invitations, you will have to make several decisions.

- ◆ RESPONSE CARDS: Stationers will show you small response cards and envelopes to enclose with the invitations, but only you can decide whether to use them. Some people consider such cards to be more suited to business or charity affairs than wedding invitations. Even when agreeing in principle, some hosts reluctantly decide to use them to assure prompt responses, especially for sit-down events. If you do NOT use response cards, an address for responses is needed. A return address on the envelope *is not sufficient*.

- ◆ CHURCH ADDRESS: This needs to be included if the church is one of many in a large city. If you include a direction card (often a very good idea), it may be engraved or printed, even though your invitation is engraved.

- ◆ CITY OR TOWN: Some invitations will be mailed out of town, so be sure to include the city or town where the festivities will take place.

- ◆ RECEPTION AND DINNER: If you are serving dinner, it is nice to state "reception and dinner" on the reception card so that people know for sure and don't make other plans.

- ◆ ENGRAVING OR THERMOGRAPHY? Thermography imitates engraving handsomely. Engraving used to be recognizable by lightly rubbing a finger over the lettering and feeling the unevenness. Thermography, however, also has raised letters at a fraction of the cost. To distinguish between the two, one must look at the reverse side to see the indentations made by the engraving plate. A fine distinction. Do not consider ordering printed invitations—not even for a moment!

At last! You are ready to order your invitations. Count the numbers on your guest list, jog your memory by double-checking all the names and then count again. Then order *more*. The largest portion of the cost is engraving the plate or setting up for thermography. The cost for an extra twenty-five or fifty invitations is minimal. Also order extra envelopes to allow for mistakes. At the same time, order your announcements if you plan to send them.

YOUR WEDDING RECEPTION: SOME PARTICULARS

A wedding reception, like any other form of entertaining, should be planned with your guests' enjoyment in mind. If everyone is invited to the reception, the bridal couple should be driven there without delay so the festivities can start promptly. Don't leave details and timing to chance and assume they all will work out well. Plan meticulously, then enjoy!

The Receiving Line

If your plans do not call for a reception, the receiving line quickly forms as guests are leaving the ceremony.

Today's brides, in the interest of a good party, sometimes forgo the receiving line altogether, preferring to have the bride and groom circulate at the reception to greet all guests. Some guests may prefer a receiving line in order to see and greet all the "players" in the beginning, so they can then relax and enjoy the reception. Others may be very thankful they do not have to stand in line interminably. The choice is up to you.

Following are the suggested receiving line positions and procedures.

1. Mother of the bride

2. Father of the bride (optional)

3. Mother of the groom

4. Father of the groom (optional)

5. Bride

6. Groom

7. Matron of honor

8. Maid of honor

9. Bridesmaids

Ushers and the best man do not stand in the receiving line. It is customary for the bridesmaids to take their positions in the line—and a pretty picture they make, indeed! Less traditionally, either for lack of space or in the interest of time, only the maid of honor stands with the wedding party.

If the bride has no mother, her father, another relative or a close friend may stand at the head of the line.

Frequently a father greets the guests before they approach the receiving line. This is fine, but fathers should position themselves far enough ahead of the receiving line so as not to be thought a part of it.

Instead of letting guests stand interminably waiting in the hot sun or cold wind to go through the receiving line, cheer them with glasses of champagne. Be sure to have a table placed where they may leave their used glasses before they go through the receiving line. Also arrange that someone—perhaps a close friend—encourages them to mingle with other guests, then reenter the line when it thins out. Some brides plan ahead to have the receiving line break up at a certain time no matter what; the choice again is up to you.

When guests reach the receiving line, they expect to say only a few words of admiration and good wishes. Greet each person cordially. Let him know you are happy he is there, then *promptly* and graciously introduce him to the next in line. Encourage your bridesmaids to do the same. By taking only a few moments, you will be doing *all* your guests a favor.

An announcer is sometimes used, but only for a

very formal wedding. He asks the name of each guest, then relays it quietly to the mother of the bride or to whoever is standing first in line. Your catering service can provide you with an announcer, or if you wish, an usher can substitute for a professional. Usually, however, one can depend upon considerate guests to help you by quickly giving their names. It also helps to review the acceptance list frequently ahead of time.

Because no one will be free to circulate among the guests until receiving line duties are finished, alert close friends or relatives to watch out for specific out-of-town friends who might be standing apart.

Gratuities

At a club, hotel or restaurant reception, the host should pay gratuities in advance to the cloakroom, rest room and parking attendants.

The Bride's Table

Even if the guests serve themselves from a buffet, it is acceptable to have a bride's table at a large wedding. The table is for the wedding party—without parents, escorts or dates, but with husbands and wives of the wedding party, if possible.

A long, narrow table is arranged with everyone seated on one side facing the room. Use place cards. The bride and groom are seated in the center—the bride on the groom's right, the best man to her right, the maid of honor to the groom's left.

The table may be decorated with flowers, white preferably. The cake may be placed in front of the bride and groom as long as it does not conceal them from their guests, or on a separate table.

If all the guests are to be seated, parents may have a special table. Traditionally the groom's parents are guests of honor, the mother seated to the right of the bride's father, the groom's father to the right of the bride's mother. Grandparents, godparents, the clergyman and his wife, and closest friends are seated at the parents' table.

Dancing

When the bride and groom are ready for their first dance, the orchestra swings into their favorite dance tune. There is a traditional dance sequence that may be followed. *(See page 60.)* Although the bride and groom will be the first to dance, they need not be the first in line when a buffet is served:

Toasting the Bride

Ask the musicians to play a fanfare so friends will gather around for the toasts and cake-cutting procedure. Just before the cake is cut, the best man toasts the bride. The groom and both fathers may then offer other toasts. The bride and groom drink to one another and to their parents. After the toasts the best man may read a few congratulatory messages.

Cutting the Cake

The bride uses a knife decorated with ribbons or flowers. Perhaps she received an engraved one as a wedding present or wishes to use a family heirloom. With the groom's hand placed on hers, the bride cuts the first slice from the lowest tier of the cake, and as a symbol of sharing their lives, she gives her husband the first bite; he gives her the next. This is a lovely custom when handled gracefully and unselfconsciously. It is not amusing to see a beautiful bride or handsome groom smeared with gooey frosting.

The cake is then cut by a waiter or waitress, or someone other than the bride or groom, and served to the guests. The top tier may be removed and saved to wrap, freeze and enjoy at your first-anniversary celebration.

Individual boxes for the guests, each containing a slice of cake, are seldom seen today. The significance of this charming favor was to place it under one's pillow and dream of one's future spouse; those already married would be granted a wish.

Throwing the Bouquet

Before leaving to change into going-away clothes, the bride—with the groom at her side—tosses the bouquet to her bridesmaids. Toss it from a stairway, an upstairs window, a balcony or any attractive raised setting. If none is available, improvise with a small platform covered in white. Sometimes other unmarried women gather to catch the significant next-to-be-married symbol. Brides also may throw a bridal garter, *modestly and tastefully* removed by the groom, to the bachelors. This is *their* next-to-be-married symbol.

Changing to Going-Away Clothes

The maid of honor accompanies the bride to help her change (see sections on duties of the maid of honor, the wedding gown and veil). Bridesmaids may follow. Ushers accompany the groom. Just before the bride and groom are ready to leave, the maid of honor notifies the parents of the bride and groom so they can have a brief, private good-bye.

Leaving the Reception

Be sure the best man has the get-away car ready and the photographer is ready for this important photograph, which may include rice, confetti or rose petals. *(See pages 48 to 49.)* This is a happy and memorable moment for you and your guests. Away you go!

Notes for a Very Small Wedding

For the bride on her own or at a very small wedding— whether at a friend's or your own apartment, home or garden—there is no recessional. When the ceremony ends, the bride and her husband turn and stand in place to receive good wishes and congratulations.

If parents are present they tend to take the same positions as in church—the bride's parents to the left, the groom's parents to the right.

Gifts and Appointments

PLANNING FOR YOUR GIFTS

After you have carefully cataloged each wedding gift as it comes in, you may want to display them. Displaying one's wedding gifts is a custom going back to the days when the bride moved straight from her family's home into her married life. This custom is infrequently practiced today, most likely because the bride is not living at home, she is working, and she has neither the space nor the time. If you should wish to display your gifts, however, especially if you are having a home wedding, here are a few pointers to follow.

To display your gifts, use card tables placed side by side or folding tables, or improvise by using sawhorses with boards or plywood on top. Cover the table with a white cloth—satin if you wish—that may be decorated with ribbon bows or artificial white flowers. You might even have your florist do a professional display table, if you are in an extravagant mood.

If you expect to receive a large number of costly gifts and the display area is to be open and available for long periods of time, you should probably see that someone is inconspicuously stationed in the room to watch over things as guests wander through.

Gift display tips:

♦ Do not exhibit CARDS of donors.

♦ Do not display CHECKS. An empty envelope or a card bearing the word "check" may be placed on the table, if you wish. This is optional.

♦ ARRANGE THE GIFTS as artistically as possible. Keep in mind the donor's feelings by the thoughtful placement of each gift. For example, a little ceramic salt-and-pepper shaker would look attractive next to your everyday pottery but would show to disadvantage near a Steuben bowl or a silver tea set.

♦ SEPARATE SIMILAR GIFTS.

♦ If you receive exact DUPLICATES, display only one. If identical gifts make a handsome pair, display them both.

♦ Try to borrow PLATE AND TRAY DISPLAY RACKS from a gift shop.

♦ When displaying dinnerware, crystal and silver, use only ONE PLACE SETTING.

♦ You may EXCHANGE DUPLICATES and unusable gifts *after* the wedding, but not at the risk of hurt feelings. With the exceptions already noted, all gifts should be displayed. You need not—in fact, *should not*—tell givers about the exchanges. Thank them for the gift they sent, not the substitute.

Sadly, guests will often bring wedding gifts to the reception, adding an extra chore for the bride and her family. (How much more thoughtful it is to send the gift ahead of time!) You must appoint someone who will be in charge of putting these gifts in a safe place at the wedding reception and arranging for their transportation home.

Much is said throughout this book about gifts—registering, receiving, exchanging, displaying, and writing thank-you letters. There are circumstances, however, when the bride and groom sincerely do not want any gifts at all. Maybe they are about to consolidate two households into one, or they have other reasons. Since the words "No gifts please" are specifically forbidden on wedding invitations, what can you do? You can tell close friends how you feel and rely on them to spread the word. If despite your wishes some friends send gifts, do not make an issue of it. Just accept graciously.

THANK-YOU NOTES

Handwritten thank-you notes are important, and you must keep up with them daily or they will become a burden instead of a pleasure. If the gift is from Mr. and Mrs. Giftsender, address your thanks to them both. Include your fiancé's name in the body of the letter

("Bob and I are looking forward to using the beautiful glasses . . ."), but sign only your own name. (The only time you sign your names jointly is on gift and greeting cards.) Use paper that is unadorned or with your own name or monogram. It is too soon to use the groom's initials or have his name imprinted with yours on the stationery.

Although you would never request money, you might be lucky enough to receive checks from relatives. The donors will be pleased if you tell them how you plan to spend the money. You might follow this thought in your own words, "We would have had to wait so long for such an elegant lamp [or whatever], but now, thanks to your generous check . . ."

A sharp warning: Some brides have the mistaken idea that their busy schedule excuses them from writing prompt thank-you notes. This myth has been the cause of many misunderstandings and consequent criticism of the bride and her family. A donor sometimes worries that the gift was never delivered and requests the store to put a tracer on it. To find "Yes, it was delivered" embarrasses both of you. When you think of the time, effort and money your friends spent on you, you will agree they have every right to expect a prompt, warm, personal letter in return.

Should gifts arrive after you have left on your honeymoon (they will), it is nice for the bride's mother or another family member to send acknowledgment cards in your absence. For example: *Your gift arrived after Jason and Lisa left on their wedding trip. One of them will write to you personally when they return.*

What about thank-you notes for shower gifts, even though you have thanked the donors at the party? Absolutely *YES*!

Here's an efficiency tip from my well-organized daughter. Having known the guest list in advance, she addressed and stamped envelopes ahead of time. After the shower, with half the work already done, she was able to concentrate on brief, enthusiastic notes. She warns, however, to be careful not to mail the empty envelopes *before* the party takes place!

If a wedding gift arrives from one of the shower guests before you have had a chance to write, you may combine your thanks for both presents into one letter.

WORKING WITH YOUR CALENDAR

Now that the wedding is fast approaching, the tempo is beginning to quicken. You will notice your calendar filling up with pre-wedding appointments of all kinds, not to mention showers and parties. Most brides today are working full-time up until a few days before the wedding, so all of this can be a bit overwhelming. Now is a good time to go over your daily calendar and pace the scheduling of all of your activities as best you can, making sure that you leave yourself some downtime. Just remember not to panic—follow the checklist, take one step at a time and it will all be done.

At this point, these are the things which should be on your calendar:

- Bridal gown fittings.

- Bridal shower dates.

- Party dates, including rehearsal dinner, bridesmaids' party, wedding day luncheon if applicable, brunch the day after if applicable, and any other parties to be given by friends.

- Bachelor/bachelorette party date.

- Jeweler appointment for the groom's wedding ring, if applicable.

- Shopping dates for your bridal party gifts, groom's wedding gift and last-minute trousseau items.

- Dentist and doctor appointments for premarital checkups and blood tests.

- Attorney appointment to make a will.

- Hair, manicure, pedicure and trial makeup appointments for the week before the wedding.

- Hair, makeup (and massage?) appointments for you and the bridesmaids (and perhaps the mothers) the day of the wedding.

- Date to go with the groom to get a marriage license.

- Food and beverage tasting at the caterer's.

- A quiet few hours with your mom, perhaps lunch and a massage?

BRIDAL SHOWERS

Lucky you! How generous and thoughtful of friends to plan a shower for you! Note the word "friends"— traditionally, close members of either the bride's or the groom's family did not give showers, as such an invitation from a family member might appear to solicit gifts, no matter how innocent their intentions. Today this is done occasionally, but if a close relative wishes to honor you, then a luncheon, tea, cocktail party or dinner would be preferable.

Unless the shower hostess plans to surprise you, which is risky business, she will discuss plans with you. Besides setting the date, she will ask you to make up a guest list, and will probably consult you on the kind of shower and the colors you prefer.

Guest Lists

Before you make your list, ask the hostess how many she would like to entertain. Insist on her giving you a specific number, and then make your list accordingly, allowing for approximately a 25 percent rate of regret. It is inadvisable to include the same people at more than one shower. Today, however, especially if the guest list is small, the bridesmaids or party hostesses may be invited to more than one shower with the firm direction that they may bring a present to only *one*. You should invite no one to a shower whom you do not intend to invite to both the wedding and the reception, but by no means do *all* wedding guests need to be invited to a shower!

Even if your future mother-in-law lives out of town, place her name on the lists for courtesy invitations. She will enjoy keeping up to date with your activities.

Have compassion for your bridesmaids' already strained budgets. Select a low-cost gift category when they will be among the guests, and whisper that old adage—that you desire their presence, not their presents.

Kinds of Showers

Before you settle on a category, consider the following list of possibilities—a few of which include the men. Best are those that allow donors to select from a wide price range. Spare yourself from criticism for asking for anything as mercenary as a "money tree"!

- KITCHEN: This is good because of the wide price range, from a potholder to a set of knives or a blender. Specify color preferences, and let the guests know where you are registered.

- BATHROOM: Specify color preferences and let the guests know where you are registered.

- RECIPES AND INGREDIENTS: This can include anything from a special herb to an appropriate mold or cooking utensil, and the gifts need not be expensive.

- **PANTRY:** This can be extravagant gourmet or essential and practical.

- **PAPER GOODS:** There are numerous innovative ideas in this category, such as cocktail napkins, guest towels and note cards.

- **ROUND-THE-CLOCK:** This invitation assigns each guest an hour of the day or night. The guest selects a gift suitable for that hour. The honoree may open the gifts in order of time, perhaps starting with an alarm clock, then a bath towel or box of soap, next a coffeepot or jam jar. This is fun!

- **AROUND-THE-HOUSE:** This is similar to Round-the-Clock, but instead of assigning times, you specify a certain room, such as the guest room, powder room, kitchen, breakfast room, patio or even garden. Although this shower may be inappropriate if the couple is moving into a three-room apartment, the gifts can be saved for their future dream house.

- **CLOSET ACCESSORIES:** The hostess will have to coordinate this one so everything will match.

- **POTS AND PANS:** This is an expensive category for individual donors, but guests may pool their resources.

- **LINENS:** This is also expensive for individual donors, but two or more guests may give jointly.

- **LINGERIE:** Lingerie can be expensive, and as such is often considered a trousseau item. Lingerie showers are fun, however, so for this theme, encourage guests to bring less expensive lingerie items such as sachets, panties or pantyhose. More expensive items—a lovely peignoir set, for instance—may be given by the bridesmaids as a group, or several guests together. Mothers of the bride and groom may also want to give an important item of lingerie.

- CRYSTAL OR CHINA: These are usually given as wedding gifts.

- MISCELLANEOUS: This type of shower is more difficult for the donor and not as much fun for the recipient.

Sometimes a groom feels left out of pre-wedding festivities, but he won't if you suggest an evening shower with gifts for him. Here are a few suggestions along that line:

- HOUSEHOLD TOOLS: Anything from thumbtacks or a measuring tape to a step stool will fit this category.

- GADGETS: There are a remarkable variety of these!

- HOUSE PLANTS and related accessories: This shower will work if these items fit your style and will not have to be transported too far. Planting supplies, pebbles, containers, plant hangers, etc., will all work.

- GARDENING TOOLS and supplies: This is appropri-

ate if you will be moving into a house with gardening space.

- ◆ GOURMET COOKING ITEMS: Many men enjoy and
  have a flair for cooking.

- ◆ BAR EQUIPMENT: This will include bar glasses, towels, openers, jiggers, wines and liqueurs.

- ◆ HOBBY SHOWER: This can relate to your fiancé's interest or hobby, such as music, fishing, sports or
  photography.

At your showers, be certain someone is listing each
gift and its donor. It is almost impossible to pair gifts
with cards later. Each gift has merit, so always thank
the giver profusely and send a thank-you note later.

Ask another helper to retrieve the ribbons and create a "bouquet" to use at the rehearsal.

Guests enjoy handling the gifts. Instead of holding
gifts up to view across the room, start each box on a
tour of the guests.

Do not let the party become so much fun that you
don't open the gifts until afterward. A shower is a
shower, and many guests will be disappointed if their
well-thought-out gift is not opened then. Be sure, however, to move along quickly with your opening of gifts.
If you spend too much time on each one, you will risk
having your guests become tired, and some may have
to leave to return to work or other responsibilities.

OTHER PARTIES

If the wedding is scheduled for late afternoon or evening, it is not unusual for a close friend to entertain the members of the bridal party, parents and out-of-town guests at a buffet lunch on the wedding day.

Even if you decide to follow the custom of not seeing the groom until the ceremony, feel free to accept. One can leave before dessert; then it will be the other's turn. An "accomplice" can phone when the coast is clear.

This tradition stems from the past when marriages were arranged—complete with dowry—by fathers of the bride and groom. It was inadvisable for the groom to see his selected bride in case he didn't like her looks and bolted!

SCHEDULE OF PARTY DATES

To simplify and clarify, send each bridesmaid a schedule of parties and the wedding week. Include:

- Reminder to break in shoes
- List of parties, with particulars
- Rehearsal time and place
- Rehearsal dinner time and place
- Where bridesmaids and ushers will lunch or dine before the wedding

- Where bridesmaids will dress

- Time and place for pre-wedding photographs

- Paring with ushers for the drive from the church to the reception, including an admonition to "please be prompt"

GIFTS FOR THE BRIDAL PARTY

When selecting gifts for your bridesmaids and other members of the bridal party, you should choose something with keepsake value. Suitable gift suggestions might be earrings, a charm, any small piece of jewelry, a picture frame or a compact, with your maid of honor attendant receiving a gift a bit more expensive than those for the bridesmaids. The gift will become even more meaningful if it is engraved with the wedding date and the recipient's initials. All of these gifts may be presented at your bridesmaids' luncheon or party, or the rehearsal dinner.

There are many bridal catalogs and websites, all of which offer innumerable choices for bridal party gifts and other wedding trinkets. These can save you much time and effort, but unfortunately many of the items are of poor quality. You may not be able to tell that from the image in the catalog or on the screen, so be very careful if you choose to select your bridal party gifts in this manner.

GIFTS FROM THE GROOM

Your fiancé's gifts for his groomsmen should follow the same principle as those for your bridesmaids, with the best man's gift being a bit more expensive than the others. Typical gifts are cuff links, a leather box, a pewter mug, a picture frame, a silver jigger, a fine desk or dresser accessory, a key chain or a travel gadget. These gifts may be given at the bachelor party or the rehearsal dinner.

HOSTESS GIFTS

Every shower or party hostess deserves to be thanked with a gift for her thoughtfulness and generosity. You may do this by sending a gift after the shower or sending a flower arrangement to use at the party. If you plan to send flowers, tell her in advance. Ask about her color scheme and where she would like to place the arrangement.

If you should bring your thank-you gift to the shower with you, be sure you do not present it to the hostess until the party is over and most of the guests have left. You would not want to compete with the gifts the others have brought just for YOU.

It's Getting Close Now!

In a sense, nothing will happen until the invitations are received. That's why our first subject is about getting them addressed and mailed. There are a variety of other important tasks described here that need to be accomplished, as well, before the final weeks.

ADDRESSING THE WEDDING
INVITATIONS

For a small wedding of fifty or fewer, you or your mother may handwrite the invitations, or use your own, a friend's or a professional's talent for calligraphy. Use plain, finest-quality fold-over paper in ivory or white. You may follow the conventional, formal wording and spacing or write a carefully worded, friendly note.

For a change of pace, let's play a game. Can you find nine mistakes in the following address?

Mr. & Mrs. Chas. D. Blake and Family
33 E. 25th Ave.
San Francisco, CA 94112

You probably spotted them all. If you did not, here are the rules for addressing:

- Write *and* between Mr. and Mrs. Symbols are not permissible.

- *Charles*, not *Chas.*; write the name in full. No abbreviations except *Mr., Mrs., Ms., Dr., Sr.* and *Jr.*

- *David*, not *D*. No initials are permissible. If you do not know what the initial stands for, omit it.

- Never *and Family*.

- Write out *East, West, North* and *South*.

- Write out *Twenty-fifth*. Use no numerals except for the house numbers and zip code.

- Write out *Avenue*. Also *Boulevard, Road, Lane, Street*, and so on.

- Spell out *California*. Again, no abbreviations.

- All envelopes must be addressed by hand, preferably in permanent black ink. Never, never use a computer, labels or a typewriter.

For the most part, wedding invitations come with two envelopes, the "outer" envelope and the "inner" envelope. The gummed *outer* envelope is the one that will be hand-addressed, stamped on the front, with the return address on the back. The *inner* envelope, ungummed, will hold the invitation and all other information, such as return cards. It is addressed with the guests' handwritten titles and family name only, and is placed inside the outer envelope.

In addition to the rules above, there are quite a few additional instructions for addressing wedding invitations. In the long run, you will be pleased that you took the time to address them properly. Use your guest list, and address carefully. Follow this guide, and check each name as you finish.

- To a husband, wife and children under eighteen:
  Outer envelope: Mr. and Mrs. Joseph Guest
  Inner envelope: Mr. and Mrs. Guest
  Elizabeth and John

- To a married couple when the wife retains her married name:
  Outer envelope: Mr. Kenneth Guest and Ms.
  (or Miss) Barbara Townsend
  (written on one line)
  Inner envelope: Ms. (or Miss) Townsend and
  Mr. Guest

- To a husband and wife:
  Outer envelope: Mr. and Mrs. Joseph Guest
  Inner envelope: Mr. and Mrs. Guest

- To a widow, or if separated:
  Outer envelope: Mrs. Robert Guest (never Mrs.
  Alice Guest)
  Inner envelope: Mrs. Guest

♦ To a divorcée who has not taken back her maiden
name:
  Outer envelope: Mrs. Barbara Guest or Mrs.
                  Barbara Townsend Guest
  Inner envelope: Mrs. Guest

OR

  Outer envelope: Mrs. Townsend Guest (this op-
                  tion is explained in the chapter
                  on invitations)
  Inner envelope: Mrs. Guest

♦ To a single woman of any age—no matter how
young:
  Outer envelope: Miss (or Ms.) Carolyn Guest
  Inner envelope: Miss (or Ms.) Guest

♦ To a single man:
  Outer envelope: Mr. Thomas Guest
  Inner envelope: Mr. Guest

♦ To two sisters:
  Outer envelope: The Misses (or Misses) Elizabeth
                  and Mary Guest
  Inner envelope: The Misses (or Misses) Guest

♦ To two brothers:
  Outer envelope: The Messrs. (or Messrs.) John
                  and William Guest
  Inner envelope: The Messrs. (or Messrs.) Guest

- To two persons living at the same address, same or different sex (if one of each, the woman's name is on the first line):

   Outer envelope: Miss (or Ms.) or Mr. First Last
   Miss (or Ms.) or Mr. First Last
   (on separate lines)

   Inner envelope: Miss (or Ms.) or Mr. Last Name
   Miss (or Ms.) or Mr. Last Name
   (on separate lines)

The title "Mr." is not used until high school age. Until a boy is eight, he may be addressed as "Master." After that, he is addressed without a title until he graduates from high school or is approximately eighteen years old. If you are uncertain on how to address a female guest, "Ms." is appropriate.

In addition to the specifics listed above, there are a few more general addressing instructions:

- Place invitations in the inner, ungummed envelope. Traditionally, folded invitations are inserted with the folded edge going in first. Envelope-sized invitations are inserted with the engraved side facing the unstamped side of the envelope.

- Enclosure cards: With envelope-sized invitations, stack the enclosed cards in this order: Place the reception card on top of the invitation. The response card, if you are using one, will come next, engraved side faceup and tucked under the flap of its own little envelope. Insert all in a unit in the manner explained above, facing the envelope flap.

- With improved printing techniques, ink no longer smudges, and protective tissues are not needed. Some true traditionalists will choose to use them anyhow.

- The inner envelope is inserted into the outer envelope upper side up, so the writing faces the *unaddressed* side of the outer envelope.

- If friends help you address, see to it that the same person addresses both the outer and inner envelopes. If return addresses are written by hand, the same hand should also write them.

- Do not lessen the impact of your classic invitation by using return address labels or computer-printed envelopes, or by adorning the envelope with decorative stickers of any kind.

- Remember to use black fountain pen or rolling ball ink—no ballpoint or felt tip.

- Professional addressers are available, many of whom specialize in calligraphy. They can be located through your stationer, a bridal shop or the classified section of your telephone book. Be sure to ask for references, and specify that they follow your instructions for addressing.

- Always mail invitations and announcements sealed, first class mail—never metered. A nice touch is a pretty stamp; some brides have enjoyed using the "Love" stamp issues for their wedding invitations.

◆ As you know, it is improper to write "and Family" on the outer or inner envelope. Equally improper is "No Children." Is there a way to keep mothers from bringing uninvited children to the reception? Yes. Telephone to suggest that they may bring their children *to the ceremony*. Explain that you must limit the number of reception guests. They will understand.

◆ Invitations should be delivered six to eight weeks before the wedding.

Here are some general instructions for addressing wedding announcements:

◆ Announcements are addressed in the same way as invitations.

◆ Announcements should be mailed *after* the wedding takes place—the same or the next day. Before the wedding you may give them to a trustworthy friend who will mail them at the proper time.

◆ No announcements should be sent to those who received invitations.

VALET PARKING, SHUTTLES AND SECURITY

Despite the added expense, there are circumstances where valet parking or shuttles are preferable, if you can manage it. These should always be *complimentary*, paid for by you in a lump sum before or afterward, tip included. When determining whether to have valet parking or a shuttle service, take the following into consideration:

+ Is your wedding in the DAYTIME OR EVENING? In a city location, guests, particularly unaccompanied females, might not want to walk to and from a parking lot after dark.

+ AVAILABILITY OF PARKING PLACES. Your wedding may be delayed if guests are circling the block at zero hour, and no guest is going to want to walk a very long distance in his/her wedding attire, especially if the weather is wet, very hot or very cold.

+ Will there be a number of ELDERLY GUESTS in attendance?

+ Think about THE PLACE your wedding is being held. If your dream location is at the top of a long hill with parking only at the bottom, be sensitive to your guests and have them shuttled to the top. To save your budget, responsible teenagers may be hired to drive safe and comfortable cars belonging to you and/or your friends. (You can have some fun with this. I attended one wedding where all the guests were shuttled in London taxis!)

+ Prepare for INCLEMENT WEATHER.

- There may be OTHER WEEKEND EVENTS for which you will also want valet parking or a shuttle service. Consider the venues for the rehearsal dinner, Sunday brunch and any other festivities connected with the wedding.

If parking *is* available at the site of your wedding, frequently it is advisable to hire someone to direct traffic. This is probably not necessary if there are delineated parking places, but if not, it is advisable in order to avoid parking jams and blocked cars. Off-duty policemen are often happy to provide this service (discuss the fee and pay ahead of time), and they will provide some security as well. If you are concerned about security, you may also want to hire guards to be present at the reception.

DRESSING FOR THE WEDDING

These days, especially at a "destination wedding," dressing for the wedding can be a party in itself for the bride and her attendants. What fun to gather together with your oldest and dearest friends as you prepare for the most important and exciting event of your life!

Someone will be needed to help you dress, unless you are wearing the simplest of wedding suits. It used to be that the bridal shop or department store where you purchased your gown would provide this service. Some do, but they are few and far between. This is a fine job for the maid or matron of honor or sister of the bride. Buttons will need to be buttoned, zippers zipped, trains will need to be checked, and the bride needs to be warned to be extremely careful not to get lipstick or makeup on her dress as she puts it on! She also should be advised not to sit ON her dress as she rides to the church, but to sit straight with her dress carefully placed around and behind her on the car seat.

Dressing for the wedding is most frequently done at one's own home, although if one is having a large home wedding, sometimes it is advisable to dress at a friend's home to avoid the confusion of the wedding setup. It is fun to arrange for your bridesmaids to arrive at the home several hours before the wedding to participate in the process of getting ready. If you want to be completely extravagant and pampered, have your hairdresser, makeup artist or masseuse (or all three!) come to your home to make you beautiful and relaxed, and all the bridesmaids, too. (Don't forget to invite your mom. She will like this, and how wonderful for her to be among the first to see her daughter in her wedding dress on her wedding day!) Be sure to have someone available to take pictures, perhaps a bridesmaid with a disposable camera.

This type of gathering is a delightful luxury, and having all that wonderful support is calming to the nerves. It is advisable for you to provide something light to eat and drink, however, especially if you dress in the late morning or over the noontime. You don't want any attendant to faint from hunger, nor do you want to yourself! Be sure to eat *something*, even if it's the last thing on your mind.

Remember that churches also often have facilities for dressing, although these might not be as comfortable as those in a home. Check them out at your preliminary church meeting. Also keep in mind the photography and the fact that you will want to complete as much of it as possible *before* the ceremony. *(See pages 55 to 56.)* The total wedding party and close relatives will need to be there for that, so keep your logistics in mind as you plan.

THE BACHELORETTE PARTY

This is a relatively new tradition that seems to be women's answer to the bachelor dinner, having evolved from the traditional bridesmaids' luncheon. You may invite your bridesmaids to a dinner (or luncheon, if you wish), or perhaps a night away on the same night as the bachelor dinner. Only your attendants need be present. This is an opportune time for good-natured bonding, to give your bridesmaids their gifts and, if the party is at home, to show them your trousseau and wedding presents. Your honor attendant may wish to help you in the planning of this, but it should be *your* party.

THE REHEARSAL DINNER

This is a party traditionally given by the parents of the groom, and it usually takes place after the rehearsal. Included in the guest list are the bridal party, their husbands, wives and fiancés, close family members of the bride and groom and special out-of-town guests.

If the groom's family gives this party, it will be their greatest—and perhaps their only—opportunity to contribute to an important pre-wedding event, and they will enjoy doing it. If the parents of the groom do not offer to give this party, it may be given by anyone, including the bride's family—away from their home, for the sake of their sanity.

- LOCATION: The party can be given wherever convenient—at home or in a club, hotel or restaurant. Even if the party takes place in a city where the groom's parents (or whoever gives the party) are strangers, advance arrangements can be made. Home clubs should be checked to see if they have reciprocal privileges with clubs in other cities. If this is not an option, the bride's parents should be consulted for recommendations, and details can be arranged by direct correspondence (mail, phone, fax, e-mail) with the hotel or restaurant of choice. Some hosts might prefer to take the trouble to visit the possible venues in person.

- WHAT TO CHECK OUT:

  * Several detailed menus from which to choose

* Wine list

* Complete prices, including pre-dinner drinks

◆ SPECIFY:

* Private dining room.

* Desired arrangements of tables such as T or U shape, or a number of smaller tables.

* Table appointments such as candles and linens.

* When flowers are ordered, be sure to agree on the cost and exactly what is wanted, because prices vary startlingly in different sections of the country. Flowers can be of any color, and any timely, romantic or colorful theme is appropriate. A gracious gesture is for the flowers to be given to the bride's parents or grandparents at the end of the party. They may be taken home or used the next day at the wedding or reception.

◆ WHOM TO INVITE: The bride needs to be consulted for her guest list. In addition to members of the wedding party, the attendants' husbands, wives and fiancés should be included, and—if the bride wishes—those special relatives and friends who will travel some distance to the wedding. Some rehearsal dinners also include close local friends and family, especially those who have entertained previously for the bride and groom. The clergyman and his wife are invited only if they are close friends of either family.

A recent trend is to have very large rehearsal dinners. By all means have the rehearsal dinner as large as you wish, but don't let it get out of hand. Keep in mind that some intimacy is lost, and paying for a big crowd can be a financial burden for the hosts. Too large a rehearsal dinner can also detract from the wedding reception the next day.

Guests will often travel long distances to attend weddings of good friends. An alternate idea to including them at the rehearsal dinner is to arrange (prepaid, if possible) a private dinner for them at another restaurant or club. Perhaps close friends who have offered to entertain for the bride and groom might welcome the suggestion to give a party for out-of-town guests that evening. The idea is to make the out-of-town guests feel welcome, and certainly they will understand your wish to keep the rehearsal dinner intimate. If it is at all feasible and the locations are close by, perhaps some of the wedding party could stop by after the rehearsal dinner.

- INVITATIONS: No matter how certain it is that everyone knows about the rehearsal party plans, be sure to send written invitations. This will avoid confusion about the time and place, and the possibility of overlooking a guest. An informal note will do, the information may be written on engraved cards, or special printed invitations may be ordered ahead of time.

- GIVING THE DINNER AWAY FROM HOME: Hosts should arrive well ahead of time to arrange place cards, check the tables and be ready to greet their guests. The party will be more successful if the seating is arranged to mingle age groups and local residents with out-of-towners. By writing names on *both* sides of the place cards, you can refresh the memories of those guests who have just met and who dislike admitting they've already forgotten each other's names.

For a large party, post a seating chart near the entrance with names written or typed in *large* letters.

♦ FOR AN AT-HOME DINNER: Perhaps enough card or folding tables can be set up to seat everyone. Again, a seating chart should be used.

The dinner plan might call for an informal buffet, with guests expected to take their plates and sit "anyplace." If it is done this way, it is thoughtful to post a chart listing groups of six, eight or ten, directing them "to the den," "on the porch," "living room around the fireplace"—wherever there is a comfortable seating arrangement and a few conveniently placed tables.

♦ TOASTING THE BRIDE: The groom's father should be prepared to give a toast. He may mention his new family-to-be, but his main words should be directed to the bride. Others will most likely toast the happy couple as well.

♦ WHAT ABOUT MUSIC AND DANCING? The party may be made as simple or elaborate as one wishes. If there is music, it should be for only a short time. Rehearsal dinners usually break up early.

- **PHOTOGRAPHS AND VIDEOS**: It is a nice surprise to engage a photographer or videographer, or to ask a friend to record the rehearsal dinner party. These pictures will be a welcome addition to the wedding album.

- **PAYING THE BILL**: At a club, the chit should be signed in advance. A service charge will be added to the bill. At a restaurant or hotel, to avoid being presented with the bill in front of the guests, arrangements can be made to:

  - Give the maître d'hôtel a credit card upon arrival, then sign the receipt away from the table.

  - Arrange a charge account ahead of time, and have the bill mailed.

  - Be quietly excused to take care of the bill while guests are drinking coffee.

- **TIPPING CAN ALSO BE HANDLED DISCREETLY**:

  - Hotel catering departments do not expect tips; arranging parties is their business.

  - One does not tip a restaurant owner.

  - Always tip the wine steward, the captain and the waiters.

  - Upon request, a hotel or restaurant will add an agreed-upon percentage to the bill to take care of gratuities, and distribute them equitably. This procedure eliminates the need for hasty mental arithmetic calculations.

* If the host patronizes the same restaurant regularly, he probably gives the maître d'hôtel a Christmas present. If this is a one-time visit, a tip will be expected.

* For an added thoughtful touch, the cloakroom and parking attendants may be tipped in advance. It should then be made clear that the attendants are not to accept additional tips; the attendants should inform the guests that the matter has already been taken care of.

One final note: The bride and groom must NOT stay late at the rehearsal dinner if it is the night before the wedding!

SPECIAL PEW HOLDERS

I cannot sufficiently stress the importance of pew arrangements. Who wants fiery-tempered relatives or awkward situations at this special time?

The bride's family and friends sit on the left side of the church; the groom's family (as guests of honor) and friends sit on the right. Send reserved-pew cards to family members and those special friends you wish to honor. Ask the groom's parents for their list, and send reserved-pew cards to their special friends, too. Such a procedure is a lovely and important step that these days is often overlooked in the flurry of activity leading up to the wedding. If you do this, you will be truly rewarded by the grateful guests who have been made to feel special by your thoughtfulness.

Reserved pews are referred to as "within the ribbons" because these rows are often identified by extra flower or ribbon decorations.

Specially engraved cards for pew holders can be purchased from stationers, although more often the bride's mother writes the information on plain cards or her engraved calling cards.

It is better to send these special pew cards *after* you receive acceptances. This way you avoid the possibility of having empty seats or the problem of rearranging the seating plan.

At a small or less formal wedding, you may dispense with sending pew cards. Just notify those honored guests by telephone. You must always inform the ushers by giving them a list of names and assigned pews. Review the list with the head usher and be sure he understands all arrangements.

On your card, engraved or plain, handwrite:

> *Pew 3—Bride's Reserved Section*
> *Mr. and Mrs. Special Guest*

> *Please present this card to your usher*

THE GUEST BOOK

You will want to select a responsible person to handle the guest book at the reception. This may be a youthful relative or a close friend. You might want to spend some time with this specially selected person purchasing an attractive guest book. This outing can be a most enjoyable time together, especially if followed by lunch and a good visit.

If you have a receiving line, plan to station her at a table ahead of it, but not too close. If there is no receiving line, try to put the table in an area that will be passed by most of the guests as they enter the reception. Provide two nice pens with the guest book when the time arrives. Do not attempt to have a roving guest book attendant. No matter how hard she tries, she is certain to overlook a few guests.

THE WEDDING PROGRAM

It is not necessary to have a program at your wedding service, but today more and more couples are choosing to do so. The purpose of the program is to guide your guests through the wedding ceremony, to let them know the names of the members of the wedding party and to provide a keepsake.

The program may be elegant and engraved, even tied with a white satin ribbon, or it may be very plain with no decoration and simply printed on a computer. A folded-over piece of heavyweight 8½" × 11" white or ivory stock is usually used, and the design should be simple and classic. The front of the program should have the names of the bride and groom (all names in the program should be listed in *full*, including middle names—no nicknames, please), the date and the place of the ceremony. A dignified line drawing of the church or another meaningful design may also be on the cover, but it should never be in color, overly ornate or "cute."

Inside you will show the schedule of the ceremony, listing the order of the music, readings, prayers, the homily and so forth. On the opposite page or the back cover you will list the total wedding party (including readers, guest book attendant, etc.) by full name. Those in the processional should be listed in the order in which they will walk down the aisle, if you know it. Here should also be included the names of the clergy and the musicians. Try to avoid using the program for personal biographies of your attendants (this can be happily done in your "weekend packet" for out-of-town guests) or for instructions of any kind. *(See pages 166 to 167.)* A short, meaningful quotation or sentiment from the bride and groom is fine if it does not dominate the program. Be sure you or the church print enough copies for each guest to have his own—no sharing, please.

SOMETHING OLD,
SOMETHING NEW

You have probably thought of it a hundred times, but because *Check List* tries to include everything, remember—you will need something old, something new, something borrowed, something blue, and a six-pence in your shoe. It is fun to understand the symbolism. The six-pence (or the shiny penny replacing it) denotes *prosperity* in your marriage. Blue denotes *faithfulness*. Borrowing shows *friendliness*. The old from your heritage combines with the new of your marriage into a *perfect union*.

The Home Stretch

In the flurry of completing everything on your list during this, the exciting last week before your wedding, you may want to refresh your memory by rereading a few appropriate topics covered in earlier sections of this book. For the most part, however, if you have diligently followed the checklist, you will be able to experience this last week and your wedding day with the serenity and joy that are your due.

Try to slow down this week. If you have kept up faithfully with your thank-you notes, here is your well-earned reward. Relax now with a clear conscience. Aren't you glad you wrote all those notes? Any more from now on can wait until you return from your wedding trip.

WEEKEND PACKETS

A wonderful and hospitable gesture, although not necessary, is the weekend packet. This is a warm "welcome" and package of information that will be waiting in the hotel room for your special guests and family who have traveled a long distance to be with you on your special day. If you wish, this can be accompanied by a small gift or basket filled with fruit or local "goodies." The following may be included in the packet, but feel free to add anything else you think might be useful:

- A schedule and description of all the wedding activities, with suggestions for appropriate attire

- Maps

- Directions and driving times

- If you are using them, schedules for buses and shuttles

- A "Who's Who" of the bridal party

- A list of recreational things to do in the area (see section on "Planning for Out-of-Town Guests")

- Recommended local restaurants or watering holes

- A personal note from the bride and groom and/or the bride's parents

THE WEDDING REHEARSAL

All the steps you've taken and the detailed plans you've made have finally brought you to this happy and important rehearsal for the main event. Afterward you will enjoy the rehearsal dinner with the bridal party, their wives, husbands, fiancés, both sets of parents and perhaps a few out-of-town guests—a very special evening.

All members of the wedding party should be present at the church, along with the clergyman, organist and other performers, and church wedding director. You will receive complete directions about everything—the processional, ceremony and recessional.

NOTE: I have deliberately omitted descriptions of specific denominations. You need be concerned only with your own, and you will have discussed details of rituals in earlier conferences with your clergyman.

Almost all of today's brides ignore the old superstition that required the maid or matron of honor to stand in for them. How much better it is to feel poised and at ease with the mechanics and ready to experience the ceremony to its fullest. This is the time to carry one of the mock bridal bouquets fashioned of ribbons collected at a shower.

There are a few rehearsal decisions to make:

- If you have both a maid and a matron of honor, you must decide which one will HOLD YOUR BOUQUET during the ceremony.

- You must decide which of your attendants will HOLD THE GROOM'S RING if you are having a double-ring ceremony.

- Should you wear a veil, decide whether you wish your honor attendant or the groom—your *husband* by then—to FOLD IT BACK at the altar.

- You may have a preference as to the STEP your bridesmaids will use in the processional. The "hesitation step" is not as popular as it once was because it is difficult to keep in perfect balance. The more natural, slow walk, in time to the music, is easier and more graceful.

- If there is to be a SOLOIST, decide at what point he/she should sing. Often this is done before the wedding march at a short ceremony, or during the ceremony at a longer nuptial mass. Ask the wedding director for an opinion.

Processional

The groom, best man and minister will enter the church from a side door and stand near the altar, looking down the aisle. The ushers walk down the main aisle in pairs. They are followed by the bridesmaids, usually walking singly and graded by height to avoid sharp contrasts. Next is the maid or matron of honor. If both are in attendance, the one chosen to hold the bride's bouquet at the altar enters immediately before the bride and her father. An exception is that the junior bridesmaid would follow the honor attendant, then the ring bearer and finally the flower girl. These three participants are optional.

I have seen unusual and pretty variations such as having the bridesmaids walk in single file up the two side aisles from the front to the rear of the church. They then follow the ushers down the center aisle.

Recessional

The maid of honor, paired with the best man, will follow the bride and groom. If there are the same number of bridesmaids as ushers, they follow in pairs. If their numbers are unequal, the bridesmaids may walk first, followed by the ushers. An alternate arrangement would be for one usher to have a bridesmaid on each arm, or vice versa. The flower girl or ring bearer may follow the bride and groom. If they have performed well, some parents decide not to tempt fate further and take them in hand at that point.

Which arm?

Take whichever arm you wish, but decide at the rehearsal. If you take your father's right arm, he can reach his pew more easily, especially if your train is long. Also, this will put you nearer the groom's side of the church walking down the aisle and closer to your own friends and family in the recessional, when you will be on your groom's right arm.

Now is the time, while you are at the church, to make sure the ushers understand about the reserved pews. If this is the ushers' first experience, remind them to ask each guest, "Friends of the bride or groom?"

Friends of the bride are seated on the left; friends of the groom on the right. However, if one family is represented by fewer guests, ask the ushers to seat the guests indiscriminately for the sake of balance.

Instruct the ushers that just before the ceremony is to begin, grandparents should be escorted to their pews. Next, the head usher will escort the groom's mother to the first pew on the right. If her son is an usher, he may do the honors. Her husband will follow a step or two behind.

The mother of the bride is the last person to be seated, escorted by the head usher, or her son, if he is an usher. No one may be seated after her. Late arrivals will have to stand in the entry until after the members of the wedding party reach the front of the aisle.

After a few seconds' pause, the music will change to the wedding march or other chosen selection. This change will herald the precise moment the processional is about to begin. The bride's mother will then stand and make a quarter turn, in time to see the first attendant start down the aisle.

Guests will follow her lead, standing and turning toward the aisle to view the procession of attendants followed by the bride on the arm of her father.

HOW MANY ARE COMING?

Your caterer will give you a "drop-dead" deadline, that is, a date when you must have a final number of acceptances for him. In most cases the caterer will give you leeway of a few numbers so you will not have to be *completely* exact, but if you have a sit-down dinner, you must come up with a number very close to the number of guests you expect to attend.

Obtaining this figure is sometimes difficult, as people can be negligent in responding to invitations. Shame on them; after *your* wedding experience I am sure you will *never* be late responding to an invitation!

Frequently it happens that there may not have been responses from a number of people, even if a response date has been indicated. If this is the case, at the last minute before the deadline you, or perhaps a member of the bridal party, will want to call these people to see if they are coming. In this way you will have to pay only for the number of guests who actually do attend. The most gracious way to do this is to say something to the effect of "Hi, Sally. I was wondering if you had received the invitation to my wedding, as I hadn't heard from you and was so hoping you would be able to come."

Unfortunately, a few people will bring uninvited children or friends. Prayer is the only defense against this.

SEATING CARDS

The guest book table can serve double duty if your reception plan includes a seated dinner or luncheon. On individual cards and their envelopes write the designated table number and name of each guest or couple. (This may be done by your calligrapher, if you wish, although the timing is sometimes difficult, as you are apt to change your seating plan up to the last minute.) These small imprinted cards and envelopes are available at stationery or bridal shops. Appoint someone (your wedding consultant, if you have one, or perhaps the guest book attendant) to arrange them alphabetically on the table, ready to distribute when the guest book is signed. To escape breezes at an outdoor reception, these cards may be held down by long satin ribbons attached to the underside of the table.

PACKING FOR THE HONEYMOON

Lay out everything to be packed; check and recheck, including your purse. Unless you are planning to reappear for brunch the next day (often couples will do this), put your honeymoon luggage in the honeymoon car the night before the wedding—all except your cosmetic case. It is a good idea to put someone in charge of that final item.

GET READY TO GO!

Now is the time to gather in one place everything you will need to wear at the wedding; bridal gear is complicated! (So is the groom's, so remind him to do the same.) Don't forget your gown, veil, underthings, two pair of pantyhose, gloves, shoes, jewelry, cosmetics, curling iron, deodorant. Think! Then put everything together. Let there be no last-minute rushing about for pantyhose or cosmetics, or a last-gasp discovery that something you need now has been packed.

YOUR WEDDING DAY

In your time chart of the wedding day schedule, be sure to *allow extra time all down the line*. If everything is done in slow motion, you will find that magically the *appearance of calmness* will actually make you *feel calm*.

This is the day of your wedding—a glorious day! Simply follow your time schedule. Bathe slowly. There will be people to help you with your dress and veil. Everything is together and ready. Take care with your makeup (a light touch is best; don't try anything dramatically startling today) and use an effective antiperspirant. Wear little or no jewelry with your wedding gown; this might detract from your own beauty—and *every* bride is beautiful. Have a box of clean tissue paper ready for the ride to the church. Place the tissue under and around your gown to keep it from mussing. You should not sit on your dress; the train should be carefully placed on the back of the car seat.

There are a few tasks in the next, "After the Wedding" chapter, and some following sections, to help with special situations.

But now it is time for the wedding. You are ready! Everyone is cheering for you. Best wishes for the happiest of days.

After the Wedding

Even when the beautiful wedding is over and the bride and groom have left, someone, usually the mother of the bride, will still have a few things to do.

Today's tradition seems to be, especially for "destination weddings," that an informal brunch or lunch be held the day after the wedding for out-of-town guests, members of the wedding party and relatives; indeed the bride and groom themselves often show up! If no relatives or friends have offered to host this event, it is gracious for the parents of the bride to do so. If the wedding is in the afternoon and no dinner is served, then this event can be a supper in the evening.

The mother of the bride must oversee the mailing of the wedding announcements the day after the wedding; this is a good project to turn over to a responsible friend.

Messages sent to the bride's parents should be acknowledged, and those sent to the bridal couple should be saved for them to acknowledge later.

The bride's wedding gown should be professionally "heirloomed" by a cleaner who specializes in preservation. He will carefully dry-clean and remove spots, enfold it in a special kind of material that does not react chemically with the fabric, and preserve the gown in an airtight container to prevent yellowing.

Handwritten acknowledgment cards to those whose gifts arrive after the bride and groom have left on their honeymoon are greatly appreciated. *(See page 134.)*

The mother of the bride should take a few days for self-pampering renewal. She might want to let the telephone or doorbell go unanswered (unless she wants to hear her friends' compliments!), and then go away for a few days.

It is a wonderful feeling of satisfaction to know that *nothing was left undone* to help the bride create that perfect wedding. Whether the bride's mother's part in the preparations was a large or small one (maybe the bride only wanted her emotional support), whether the wedding was an extravagant catered affair for hundreds of guests or a small gathering where home-baked cake was served, it was an equally joyous occasion.

The mother of the bride knows that her part was done with love and for love. What more is there?

Home/Garden Weddings

A wedding at home or in your garden can present its own complications, logistical and otherwise, especially if your guest list is on the large side. This chapter, in conjunction with other information found in *Check List*, will help you deal with these complications. There is nothing warmer or lovelier than a home wedding, so if that is your inclination, *go for it*—but read on.

People *love* to attend home weddings. Somehow the essence of a bride and groom is clearer in the home setting; there always are a certain personalized charm and joy that transcend anything one might find in a hotel, hall or private club. Finally, one cannot help but forgive those lovable souls who simply want to see your home and how you live!

Overriding all of this are many challenges, but despite these I should never wish to discourage anyone who would like to have a home/garden wedding. As far as I am concerned, every bit of frustration is more than worth it. Don't expect, however, to save money by having your wedding at home. Beyond the very simplest celebration, the cost of a lovely home wedding adds up to about the same cost as a lovely club or hotel wedding.

WILL IT WORK?

This depends, of course, on many variables.

♦ Is the AVAILABLE SPACE large enough to hold the number of guests you would like to attend?

♦ Do you live in an area where you can predict with a modicum of accuracy that there will not be a tornado, blizzard or windstorm on the day of the wedding? Can you arrange for a LAST-MINUTE RAIN PLAN?

♦ Can you solve LOGISTIC PROBLEMS such as proper parking and transportation to your home?

♦ Are you or your parents willing to make certain SACRIFICES? Here are some examples:

  * Moving out furniture to provide extra space

  * The loss of privacy for over a week

  * Risking the ire of your neighbors because of traffic or noise

  * A bedraggled lawn, stained carpets, one or two broken something-or-others

  * Boarding the pets

* Overlooking certain idiosyncrasies in your home (you *don't* have time to remodel the whole downstairs!)

* Starting close to a whole year earlier to plan for your loveliest garden ever

* Having very little use of your own home, other than sleeping there, during the wedding weekend

* Having everything *neat* and put away by reception time, upstairs bedrooms included

If you can answer positively to all of the above—or even most of the above—and you are really committed and willing to follow the information found in *Check List*, then yours will be a beautiful home/garden wedding.

SOME FIRST STEPS

If your wedding is going to have more than a few dozen people, the first thing you must do is ENGAGE A COMPETENT BRIDAL CONSULTANT, or at least someone to assist you. *(See pages 28 to 32.)* Even though you may have your own vision—indeed, you probably do if you have decided to attempt such a project—you will need someone to help you at zero hour. Clubs and hotels usually have such a person on staff; you don't, so you must hire your own. This person should be communicating with you from the beginning and should be kept abreast of what is going on. In this way, you can turn something over to him/her to complete if need be, such as transportation logistics, finding the right Porta Potties to rent, directing guests to their tables at the reception or overseeing the dance sequence. You may also hire a consultant to do the whole thing, saving you from much effort and many worries; the choice is yours. If your wedding is to be small and intimate, a good friend to help you on the wedding day could be all you need.

The second thing you should do early on (eight to ten months in advance), for a larger wedding, is to SCHEDULE A PRELIMINARY PLANNING MEETING with your consultant, the caterer, the rental company representative, the lighting company representative, a band representative and the florist—all together, if possible. This meeting may be your most important of all. It will set the tone for the wedding, determine the number of guests you can fit comfortably into the allotted space, and iron out general details of décor in terms of lighting, rentals and flowers. These people enjoy bouncing ideas off each other, a fact that will act in your favor and a good reason to meet with as many of them as possible at the same time. (Coffee and refreshments are always a nice touch at this meeting.) Items to consider include:

- The NUMBER OF TABLES that can be fit into the allotted space. (The caterer can tell you how close they can be for the wait staff to serve properly.)

- The AMOUNT OF SPACE that will be needed for the band, including a stage. Where will the band be placed? What about amplifiers for the music?

- Will you have a TENT, or tents? How large, and of what design? Clear or opaque? (Catalogs are available.) If you wish to wait and see what the weather will be, you will still have to pay a fee to reserve the tent, and then you must make the call as to whether you'll use it, approximately three days before the wedding!

- What kind of FLOOR will you have under the tent? A safe terrain must be kept in mind at all times. Your own lawn, implanted with a dance floor, is fine if it is level enough for the tables and your female guests are good-natured about their high heels sticking into the grass. Otherwise you will need to build a platform, no small feat if the tent is a large one. If you are covering a swimming pool, you can plan to be under construction for most of the week before the wedding.

- The platform will need to be covered. Black FLOOR COVERING is less expensive than green; in most cases there are so many beautifully appointed dining tables under the tent that the floor is not that noticeable.

- Will you want the TENT POLES wrapped in a coordinating color or decorated with vines and/or flowers?

- Will you need to rent BOXWOOD PLANTS to line the edge of the platform, or for fill-in elsewhere?

- Will you need a GENERATOR? Lights, music, speakers, coffeepots—they all use a great deal of electricity.

- Where will you have COCKTAILS prior to dinner? Will there be MUSIC there?

- Where will you place the GUEST BOOK TABLE? Will it need flowers?

- Where will guests leave their WEDDING GIFTS?

- Where will you have the CAKE TABLE? Will it need flowers?

- What kind of LIGHTING will you have? Pinpoints? Floods? What will you want lit? Outdoors is lovely, but it looses all of its charm when it gets dark if your guests can't see. In addition to the tent, you will want to consider lighting the wall of your house, trees, hedges, behind the stage, etc. Walk around your home at night sometime before the meeting and look at possible lighting areas.

- Will you need PORTABLE TOILETS? How many? (You will need four to five bathrooms for 250–300 guests.) Where will they be placed? (Remember you can have fun with the decoration of these, especially if you rent the deluxe models complete with lights and a sink. Oriental rugs may be laid outside, gardenias in a bowl placed on the countertops along with paper hand towels imprinted with the date and names of the bride and groom, wreaths hung on the doors, etc. Use your imagination!)

- At this meeting you can also look over the CHOICES OF RENTAL ITEMS from the rental company's catalogs: china for the reception dinner, tableware, linens, chairs (gold are more expensive to rent than white painted ones), round or oblong tables, etc. Final choices for these can be at a later date.

- Where will the BAND go for their BREAKS AND DINNER?

- If the band deposits their INSTRUMENTS at your home the morning of the wedding, will they be PROTECTED from the hot sun or rain?

- Consult with the caterer as to a later DATE FOR A FOOD TASTING OR MENU CONSULTATION and with the florist for a later DATE FOR A FLORAL CONSULTATION.

As the months roll by following this first, most important get-together with everyone, you or your consultant will be the focal person in dealing with all of them, and you will frequently be in contact.

The third thing you must do in these early months is plan for your garden. If you have a gardener, meet with him or your landscape designer immediately, as some of the preliminary steps may need to be started right away. What you plan is up to you, but keep in mind the total look you want on the day of the wedding. If the tent is going to hide a flowerbed or two, for heaven's sake don't worry about that part of your garden! Measure carefully where the tent will go, including its height, and plan accordingly. You may have to cut back a tree branch or two, plant some extra lawn seed, clear out a visible hillside or give extra water to a stressed area. Other items to consider are:

- ROUGH-HEWN AREAS that may need some help with edgings and ground coverings, such as tree bark.

- Replacing and moving of POTTED PLANTS, outdoor benches, woodpiles, etc.

- NEW PLANTINGS that hopefully will mature in time. Make provisions for their feeding, pruning, dead-heading and watering.

- Fixing up and refreshing any NEGLECTED FLOWER BED, rock garden or visible corner of your garden.

- NEW PLANTS that will be placed underground IN THEIR POTS, for color, at the last minute.

- Do you need to consult a TREE SERVICE for pruning?

Next, in these early months, you will need to give some consideration to the dresses worn by the bride, bridesmaids and mothers of the bride and groom. Keep in mind that the gowns and dresses for a garden wedding, even if the wedding is black tie, are simpler and much less ornate than those for an elegant black-tie club or hotel wedding.

If you plan to remove some of your furniture to make more room in your house, now is the time to contact and reserve a reputable moving service to hold your furniture on a truck the day and night of the wedding, to be returned the next day, if possible.

ADDITIONAL DISCUSSIONS
WITH THE CATERER

A section on catering may be found earlier in this book. *(See pages 42 to 49.)*

Additional discussions should include:

- Provisions for an extra EMPTY DINING TABLE to be used for unexpected guests, if you think you might have some.

- MENU (buffet or seated), hors d'oeuvres (passed and stationed), drinks, wine, and corkage fees if you provide your own wine.

- A simple DINNER MENU AND SOFT DRINKS FOR THE BAND, photographer and assistant, lighting people, traffic director and guard, if you use them.

- CUT-OFF DATES for when they will need to set up the tables in the tent for dinner (usually two days early) and when they will want to set up in the kitchen (usually the day before).

- The provision of a SEATING CHART and attractive stand-up or folded cards with NUMBERS FOR THE TABLES. (Some brides let their calligrapher do this.)

- Servers with champagne and waters on trays to GREET GUESTS AT THE GATE as they arrive? (A nice touch, especially if you plan to have a receiving line.)

- Drop-dead date for a FINAL GUEST COUNT. (Usually it's a week before the wedding.)

ADDITIONAL DISCUSSIONS WITH THE FLORIST

A section on florists may be found earlier in this book. *(See pages 49 to 52.)*

Additional discussions should include:

- In addition to all the flowers and decorations, will you need a RIBBON BARRIER to block off a stairway or other area where you do not wish guests to wander? (They *will*, otherwise!)

- If your wedding ceremony is at a church, will you want the florist to bring some of the CHURCH FLOWERS TO BE UTILIZED AT THE RECEPTION? If so, this must be done quickly and cleverly so the guests will not see the florist as he puts the flowers in place.

- A CHART of exactly where you would like flowers. In addition to the usual table décor, mantels and doorways, don't forget odd but prominent little corners such as fence posts, banisters, lavatories, tent poles, stationary bars and food stations—and the cake knife. Perhaps you would like a floral arch-way from which to make your entrance!

ONGOING ITEMS FOR DISCUSSION WITH YOUR BRIDAL CONSULTANT AND/OR YOURSELF

- Will you need an ALL-DAY TRAFFIC DIRECTOR for purveyors' deliveries, as well as guests?

- If your road is narrow, are you sure all TRUCKS AND VANS OR BUSES CAN NAVIGATE it and will not block it?

- Do you have ADEQUATE PARKING SPACE for the members of the band, the catering staff, setup people and all purveyors, as well as your guests?

- Will you need a STAFF PARKING SIGN? Will you need shuttles for the staff and guests? Will you need parking attendants? Is there adequate parking at the wedding ceremony site? If you shuttle guests, can their cars be left at the ceremony site all evening?

- If you have guests shuttled in, be sure to hire a reliable service that will run long enough to accommodate early and late departures. *(See pages 105 to 107.)*

- Will you want a PROFESSIONAL GUARD to watch over wedding gifts—and the guests? (An off-duty policeman is a good idea if you have a large crowd.)

◆ Who will COORDINATE THE TIME SEQUENCE of the reception, i.e., is the band ready, are the caterers ready, what will the band play and when (fanfares for toasts, the first dance, etc.)?

◆ What about GENERAL OBSERVANCE AND TROU-BLESHOOTING, such as glitches in the seating arrangements, more champagne needed for toasts, passing the word on cake cutting, care and keeping of your newly flower-bedecked antique wedding cake knife, gathering the bridesmaids when the bride is ready to change, etc.? *Someone* needs to take responsibility for these things!

◆ If there are trucks or buses near the wedding site, make sure they turn off their BACK-UP BEEPERS.

◆ Remember to turn all your telephone bells to low, and ask your on-site team (including catering staff, musicians and photographers) to TURN OFF THEIR CELL PHONES.

◆ When doing your guest seating, it is a good idea to put the YOUNGER GUESTS nearest the dance floor.

All of this might sound complicated, but if you truly want a lovely home/garden wedding, it will be accomplished by following this guide and giving yourself enough leeway for the myriad details.

ITEMS FOR YOUR OWN ONGOING
CONSIDERATION

Think about each of the following and effect or discard it as you wish:

* You may want to arrange for someone—a relative, friend, neighbor, teenager or housekeeper—to be in the house at all times the last few days before the wedding and during the wedding ceremony. He or she can be a GOFER OR TROUBLESHOOTER, ready to take on any unexpected task, large or small, as needed. (Think watering, walking the dog, answering the doorbell and the telephone, polishing that last piece of silver, moving things out of sight, making sandwiches and coffee, running errands, security and just *being* there *in case!*)

* A DAILY RIDER ON YOUR HOMEOWNER'S INSURANCE POLICY to cover any liability the week of the wedding.

* Sending NOTICES about the wedding TO ALL NEIGHBORS within earshot, as well as the sheriff or police department. Mention the band, the time the music will play and end, and cordially ask for their forbearance. Many outdoor party celebrations have been cut short because uninformed neighbors have called the police department to complain about the noise. It is always helpful to have your neighbors *on*

your side. If you have extra flowers left over the day after the wedding, a lovely gesture would be to deliver them to your neighbors' doorsteps.

- HIRING AN ELECTRICIAN, or someone familiar with your home electrical circuits, to be present throughout the complete wedding reception. The extra added voltage you will be using could—horrors—cause a blackout or kitchen failure.

- Planning A PLACE away from your home FOR THE BRIDE AND BRIDESMAIDS TO DRESS and for the wedding party to be photographed *prior* to the wedding. *(See pages 53 to 58.)*

- CHANGING YOUR HOUSE CLEANING HELP'S REGULAR SCHEDULE, if necessary, to accommodate the wedding.

- Reminding yourself at the PROPER TIME TO TURN OFF THE LAWN SPRINKLERS several days before the wedding, or whenever necessary. You do not want the grass to be "mushy," nor do you want to sprinkle the unsuspecting people who are setting up for your reception.

- MOVING YOUR CAR(S) to a neighbor's house so that your garage may be utilized the day of the wedding.

- REMODELING: nothing *major*, please! You simply cannot plan for unavoidable delays and mistakes—and no one will notice, anyway. (Bathrooms and kitchens are the very *worst* to deal with!)

And one last matter for your consideration . . .

• If you are to be married in a church with the reception at home, DO NOT LET ANYONE LEAVE HOME FOR THE CEREMONY AFTER YOU, unless he/she is well versed in all that you have planned! Many a well-meaning "helper" has changed things carefully orchestrated by you (such as removing a lovely display of antique Limoges boxes in the lavatory), thinking he/she is being helpful.

If Your Parents
Are Divorced

Divorced parents have been advised over and over again to resolve or forget their differences and to conceal any antagonistic feelings. They will be admired if they consider the bride's feelings on her important day and handle their roles with dignity, cooperation and apparent ease.

What is seldom mentioned, however, is the bride's responsibility to help ease a difficult situation. If she is mature enough to marry, she is surely mature enough to be sensitive to her divorced parents' feelings. If her parents are friendly, she will have no problem. If they are not, she should be realistic and accept the fact that she cannot act out a fairy-tale version that does not exist.

For example, if the bride's father refuses to give the bride away unless the "other woman" attends, and if the bride knows this would be unbearable for her mother, then the bride should ask a brother, godfather, grandfather, uncle or friend to do the honors. If the remarriage of the bride's mother is of long standing, and the bride is closer to her stepfather than to her natural father, she might ask her stepfather to give her away.

Although situations vary wildly, fortunately there are solutions or compromises for every problem. If financing the wedding should become the bride's sole responsibility, she should simplify it into an affordable plan.

INVITATIONS

An experienced stationer will have suggestions and samples for consideration. A desire for harmony should always be the guide.

- The parent who is closest to the bride usually issues the invitations. Grandparents, a brother or sister, or other relative may take over the honors if circumstances demand.

- If the mother of the bride has remarried, she may send the invitations as "Mrs. New Husband's Name requests . . ." or "Mr. and Mrs. New Husband's Name request . . . at the marriage of *her* daughter . . ." (giving the daughter's *full* name).

- Sometimes an envelope contains both the mother's invitation to the wedding and the father's invitation to the reception, along with the desired response address. He may give his daughter away at the altar. If he has remarried, his wife's name may appear with his on the reception invitation as host and hostess.

- If the parents are separated but not legally divorced, they should ignore their differences and issue invitations under the normal procedure.

- If the mother has not remarried and issues the invitations, she uses her divorced name. Reread the section on ordering invitations and announcements. *(See pages 116 to 123.)*

THE REHEARSAL DINNER

The rehearsal dinner presents another possible snag. It is customary for both parents to attend. Again, if they are friendly there is no problem. Talk over difficult situations in advance to find the least awkward solution. Perhaps carefully arranged place cards will satisfy, although in extremely sensitive cases, one or the other parent may decline the dinner invitation.

SEATING IN CHURCH

- The mother of the bride sits in the first pew on the left as you face the ceremony. If she has not remarried, she may sit alone or invite a relative to join her—but not a casual escort. If she has remarried, her new husband will have been escorted to her pew earlier, and she may walk out with him after the recessional. As an alternative, the head usher or her usher-son may return to escort her. Her new husband will follow immediately behind.

- After giving the bride away, her father sits in the second or third pew on the left as you face the ceremony, with his parents or his wife if she attends.

- If the groom's parents are divorced, the same seating arrangements apply to them, but on the right-hand side of the aisle as you face the ceremony.

RECEIVING LINE SUGGESTIONS

- If the bride's mother gives the reception, she stands in the line. The bride's father attends as a guest and does not stand in the receiving line. If the bride's mother has remarried, her husband does not stand in line; he acts as host.

- If the bride's father gives the reception, remarried or not, he may relinquish his place in the line to the bride's mother—a happy solution. If he has not remarried, the bride's mother may stand in the line either next to him or separated by the groom's parents. If he has remarried, he may stand first in the line. His wife does not stand in the line; she acts as hostess. The bride's mother is a guest.

Here Comes the Bride—Again

You can hardly wait to share your joy with the world. But pause a moment! If you or your fiancé has children, they should be told first, along with both sets of parents. If you are a widow, tell your parents-in-law before they hear the news from outsiders. If you are divorced, be certain to tell your former spouse, and also your former in-laws if you have kept in touch with them. Next, tell your close friends, and the news is guaranteed to travel with rocket speed.

Provided neither of you is waiting for a divorce to become final, you might announce your engagement at a dinner, tea or cocktail party, or simply at a family dinner. *(See pages 18 to 26.)*

Please disregard the information about formal newspaper engagement announcements, as it applies to first marriages only. An item about your wedding plans might appear, however, in a news column, which differs from a formal engagement announcement.

You may certainly wear an engagement ring when both divorces are final.

YOUR GENERAL PLAN

How remarkable that no two weddings are ever identical, nor should they be! Each is unique! The guidelines are here to give you help, reminders, alternatives, a smattering of advice—but only a minimum of rules. Select the items that have meaning for *you*. You might or might not want to incorporate the symbolic traditions of something old, something new, something borrowed, something blue and a six-pence in your shoe. *(See page 165.)*

Circumstances vary too much to advocate a single pattern for all second weddings. If you analyze your particular situation, your wedding plans will begin to fall in place. Consider your category: Are you a young widow? A young divorcée? A mature widow? A mature divorcée? Was your marriage annulled? Is this your second marriage but your fiancé's first? Is he much older than you are? Younger? Have you children? Has he? Young or grown? Has your former spouse remarried? Are relations amicable? Are finances a consideration? Is it your first marriage but your fiancé's second? Answer: Plan any style wedding that pleases you both.

While you and your former husband were separated, he died. Are you a widow or divorcée? Answer: a widow.

Are you about to remarry your former husband? Suggestion: Quietly is best.

Thinking about *your* specific situation will help you focus on what is best for *you*. The differences between the wedding of a young widow and that of a mature widow are quite apparent. If you are very young, you might want your father to give you away once again at a fairly sizable gathering. The mature widow would probably feel more comfortable inviting only families, children and close friends.

You have much to think about:

- Strive for a COMPLETELY DIFFERENT ATMOSPHERE from your previous wedding: different location, music, decorations, cake, dress, everything.

- YOU MIGHT PREFER AN INTIMATE CEREMONY, followed by a LARGE RECEPTION the same day or at a later date.

- If you eloped or arranged a nontraditional wedding the first time, you may yearn to savor the experience of a glorious, TRADITIONAL CEREMONY. If so, you will find many beautiful bridal gowns in a more sophisticated style than you would have chosen as a younger bride.

- Some couples delight in SURPRISING FRIENDS. You could take off to a faraway place to marry, and celebrate with a party after you return home. Instead of sending formal wedding announcements, why not notify friends by postcard from your wedding locale?

- Another surprise suggestion: Invite friends to a PARTY—NOT A RECEPTION. When guests arrive, they will find to their surprise that they are celebrating your marriage that just took place earlier that day—or which will take place right there at the party!

- Have you always heard that one should wait at least a year to marry if either is widowed? A younger couple is more inclined to wait, while some older couples might decide, based on their experiences, that life is already too short. In either case, POSTPONE ANNOUNCING YOUR ENGAGEMENT until close to the wedding date.

WHO WILL OFFICIATE?

Throughout this book I have used the word "clergyman" to cover officials of all denominations, whether they be priest, rabbi, minister, pastor or other. One can also be married by a judge, governor, chaplain, registrar, justice of the peace or ship's captain, to name a few.

Before forming even a tentative plan, make an appointment, along with your fiancé, to meet with your clergyman. *(See pages 37 to 38.)* Although the items discussed apply to church weddings, most information serves equally well for second weddings, and in locations other than churches. Check the items you wish to consider.

If you find that the clergyman is restrained by church tenets from officiating at a marriage of divorced persons, or those of different religions, he might still be able to refer you to someone who will gladly perform the ceremony. Others will bless a marriage in a meaningful rite after it has taken place.

Some churches restrict the location of the ceremony to the clergyman's study, or to a side chapel, while others permit the use of the main altar. If your guest list is small and the church is huge, you might inquire about seating your guests in the choir stalls. You probably will not need to reserve the church for a rehearsal for this simplified plan.

A SMALL WEDDING

If your previous wedding was large and lavish, this time you might decide to limit the guests to family members and close friends—perhaps no more than fifty. The ceremony could take place in a church, club, hotel or in your own or a friend's home, apartment or garden.

Small does not mean dull or somber. Small, in this event, means intimate, personal, joyous, warm and *very special*.

The Bride's Dress

Select an outfit appropriate for the season and time of day, in a becoming color or off-white. You will look glorious!

- No formal wedding gown or wedding veil

- A pretty silk or wool suit for a morning wedding

- A street-length dress or outfit for an afternoon wedding

- Long or short cocktail dress for an evening candlelight ceremony

- No gloves or hat at a home wedding

- Flowers to complement your outfit

Attendants

Instead of thinking "maid or matron of honor," or "bridesmaid," think "attendant-witness." At a small wedding, that is what both you and your fiancé need. You might ask a sister, your best friend or the friend who introduced you to your husband-to-be, or as suggested later in this chapter, your child could do the honors. Perhaps your attendant's wardrobe already includes an appropriate dress in the same degree of dressiness as yours, and in a compatible color.

Rehearsal and Rehearsal Dinner

At your initial meeting with the clergyman, perhaps he saw no need for a rehearsal. Even so, you need not forgo a festive dinner one or two evenings before the wedding. This is an ideal time for you and your fiancé to gather together your families and out-of-town guests. A thoughtful relative or friend might volunteer to host the affair. Otherwise, you and your fiancé can give the party yourselves.

Even if the party is small, ask someone to take photographs for you to add to your wedding album.

Receiving Line Following the Ceremony

At a small wedding there is seldom a processional or a recessional. You and your husband will turn and stand in place after the ceremony. Your guests will come forward to greet you.

Flowers

Flowers always add warmth and beauty to the décor. To avoid a possible disappointment, choose a florist whose work you have seen and admired—one whose suggestions are compatible with your taste.

Photographs

Be sure to record this day of days. Either ask a friend to take the pictures or engage a photographer. *(See pages 53 to 58.)*

What to Serve at Your Small Wedding

Your menu can be as special and festive as you wish.
Let your imagination and talents soar to new heights!

Music

Music always adds to the enjoyment. Suggestions: violin,
guitar, zither, accordion, piano or an organ rented for the
day. At home, if you want to keep it simple, why not enjoy your favorite CDs? You can set them up in advance.

A LARGE RECEPTION

As suggested earlier, you may wish to have a large
reception either immediately following an intimate
ceremony or at a later date. When making your plans,
consider this not as a repeat performance but a completely new one. Call upon your ingenuity.

In this book you will find detailed information on
cocktail parties and wedding receptions. Check the
items that suit your plan. You would probably decide
to dispense with the bride's table and to reduce the receiving line.

Wedding Cake

Here is your opportunity to be creative—with the help
of a master pastry cook to carry out your original ideas.

Your cake may be artistically decorated with fresh or icing flowers in your favorite colors, or you may substitute an entirely different dessert. Decorated petit fours, éclairs or flamed crêpe suzettes are possible choices.

Dancing

You and your husband will want the first dance together, but if you wish, you may disregard the rest of the traditional routine.

Catering

If you make reservations for your reception in a club, hotel or restaurant, its catering service will take care of you. If you plan to hold the event elsewhere, check the section on hiring a caterer to select the items that apply to your plan. *(See pages 42 to 49.)*

Photographers

Earlier in this book there is a section on photographs and videotapes. Select from all those reminders to assure that nothing has been forgotten. *(See pages 53 to 58.)*

INVITATIONS AND ANNOUNCEMENTS

Your choice of invitation will depend upon the size of your wedding. A general guide to traditional invitations may be found earlier in this book, outlining the conventional formulas for small, informal weddings and for larger weddings and receptions. *(See pages 116 to 123.)*

Decisions must have been easier in the "olden days" when rigid rules of etiquette forbade formal weddings for second-time brides, and the majority of those remarrying preferred a smaller wedding followed by a larger reception. Maybe in this century new customs will be born. At this particular time, you already have a number of options.

Invitations

- For a small wedding, handwritten or telephone invitations are customary. Calligraphy is another attractive option. Please, no e-mail invitations.

- For a wedding reception, invitations may be engraved or thermographed. *(See pages 122 to 123.)*

- Parents may issue the invitations for a young second-time bride, using the standard format for a church wedding:

Mr. and Mrs. Bride's Parents
request the honour of your presence
at the marriage of their daughter
(given name/maiden name/married name[if retained])
Barbara Townsend Long
to
Mr. Jeffrey Paul Fowler, Jr.
(no initial)
etc.

- For a wedding not in a church, or for the wedding reception:

    Mr. and Mrs. Bride's Parents
    request the pleasure of your company
    at the wedding reception of their daughter
    etc.

- If the bride and groom issue their own invitations, the formal style for a young bride's church wedding is as follows:

    The honour of your presence
    is requested at the marriage of
    (given name/maiden name/married name)
    Barbara Townsend Long
    to
    Jeffrey Paul Fowler, Jr.
    etc.

- For a wedding not in a church, or for the wedding reception:

    The pleasure of your company
    is requested at the marriage of
    etc.

- An older widow usually uses her full married name, such as Mrs. Kenneth Lindsay, and "Mr." prefaces the groom's full name.

- The older divorcée uses one of two forms: Mrs. (Maiden Name) Jones or Mrs. Jane Jones. Invitations include the date but not the year.

Announcements

- Parents may make the formal announcement of a young bride's second wedding, using the formula "Have the honour of announcing . . ."

- The bride and groom may make their own announcement by following the same name formulas given above for invitations.

- Announcements include *both* the date and the *year*, whereas invitations do not use the year.

- Christmas or other holiday cards can carry the message of a recent marriage.

- Personal notes to friends at a distance are the most appreciated.

- Newspaper announcements can spread the news. Fill out and send the wedding forms or compose your own message to your local paper, and to others where you and your fiancé have connections. Some newspapers will print these notices only if their own forms are used. *(See pages 87 to 89.)*

YOUR CHILDREN AND HIS

This is such a happy time for you and your husband-to-be; you want it to be happy for your and his children as well. Your relationship with them depends on many variables such as the children's ages, other parents and individual personalities and situations. Because of those differences, it is impossible to set rules of procedure to cover every person or situation.

Your wedding can be a unifying family affair if you both include the children in your plans as much as possible—a prelude to your future happiness. Here are a few ideas directed toward this goal:

- Some couples, with the clergyman's approval, write vows that INCLUDE THE CHILDREN IN THE CEREMONY.

- If you have a child mature enough to understand and accept your marriage, perhaps he or she can STAND WITH YOU during the ceremony. Occasionally a grown son will walk with his mother and "give her away."

- VERY YOUNG CHILDREN can participate by carrying out small tasks. They can show guests where to hang their coats, or attend to the guestbook, or even pass small trays of canapés.

- Children might want to JOIN THE DANCERS at the reception. If they are in their early teens and weren't exposed to dancing school, give them the opportunity to learn a few basic steps from your era. You can provide a dance teacher briefly at the rehearsal dinner, or sign them up for a short series of lessons at a dance studio, if they would enjoy it.

You remember the fairy tale about Cinderella and the "wicked Stepmother." Comic strips and joke books love to play up that same stepmother situation. You and the children will surely recognize those stories for what they are—fairy tales and fiction. Discard them forever, and relish every moment with your expanded family.

BUSINESS MATTERS

Today's bridal couples frequently pay for their own weddings—not only those marrying for a second time, but also first-timers who are already independent.

A quiet, frank discussion about finances should take place before you say, "I do." Sit down together with pencil and paper, and calmly delve into your personal and business matters in detail—"mine, yours and ours."

It is important, however, before you can take final action on certain of the subjects, to decide what name or names you will use. *(See pages 107 to 110.)* Please pay special attention to the section on the legal use of two or more names.

If you both work or have separate incomes, consider each of the items listed below.

- Decide which of you will be responsible for PAYING SPECIFIC BILLS, such as household, clothing, entertainment, children's education, insurance, and travel.

- Have you each made out a NEW WILL or trust?

- Will your BANK ACCOUNTS be separate, joint or both?

- Check the NAMES AND ADDRESSES on insurance policies, stocks, properties and other legal papers.

- PREMARITAL AGREEMENTS concerning the disposal of one's assets are frequently in order for second marriages, or for established brides and grooms. Sometimes this is a touchy, hurtful subject, whether requested by the groom or bride. Neither one should sign an agreement until each has consulted his or her own attorney. Joint advice from a single source is inadvisable. Once reconciled to the satisfaction of both of you, put the matter out of sight and out of mind.

GIFTS

All brides are cautioned time and time again to write prompt, enthusiastic thank-you notes. The second-time bride should show *twice as much* appreciation, knowing the gift came from the heart.

Are you concerned that friends might feel obligated to send gifts when they receive your wedding announcement? Don't worry; even an announcement for a first wedding does *not* call for a gift. Wedding invitees will undoubtedly send gifts; other friends might or might not.

If you are in the midst of weeding out, and trying to consolidate two households into one, you might sincerely *not* want anything more added to your already crowded household. It would be so simple and convenient to include the words "No Gifts," but etiquette frowns on using that expression on wedding invitations, while permitting it on invitations to anniversary and birthday parties. The only solution is to tell a few close friends and ask them to "pass the word along." Obviously you will not register gift selections.

If, despite your caution, some friends send gifts, just accept them graciously.

Some brides, however, might be delighted to receive presents. Following is a list of selections for the "over-supplied."

Gifts for the Bride Who Has Everything

Anything with the bride's new initials or monogram: place cards, cards, score pads and table covers for playing bridge, address embosser, initialed or name-and-address letter paper, name-imprinted invitation forms, bar glasses, towels, bed linen, table linen.

Gifts Instead of Silver

Decorative bowl, small art object, brocade or leather scrapbook, picture frame, table easel for picture, small table clock, gourmet basket, equipment for a favorite sport, addition to a hobby or a collection, health club membership, magazine subscription that highlights a couple's interests.

Gifts for a New Home

Gold house key, houseplant, garden shrub or tree, garden furniture or accessory, barbecue or hibachi.

Gifts if You Know a Bride's Household and Tastes

State-of-the-art electronic appliances or gadgets, replacement of everyday dishes and glassware.

Non-gifts to Honor the Couple

Donation to a charity in a couple's names, a group community service workday for children or the elderly (install needed playground equipment in a school, or plant a garden for a park or convalescent hospital).

A relative who might like to give a check could send a gift certificate instead.

SHOWERS

Showers are less often a part of the second-time wedding. If your same set of friends attended showers before your first marriage, they might say, or at least think, "Enough is enough."

A second-time bride was recently given this dreadful, unsolicited advice: "If nobody offers to give you a shower, give one yourself." Fortunately the bride knew that not even a relative should give a shower for her. But nothing should stop friends from entertaining at just-for-fun parties. They are the best kind!

CHECKLIST FOR A NEW START

Setting Aside Old Memories

Whether you are moving to a new home or staying in your own, plunge into a thorough, ruthless housecleaning—or rather, house clearing. It will take days to go through your papers, and every drawer and closet, so start this project immediately.

- Out of consideration for your new husband-to-be, remove your former husband's PICTURES from prominent locations. You could hang them in the children's room.

- Pack, label and store old PHOTOGRAPH ALBUMS.

- Remove from sight or discard mementos such as sentimental birthday or anniversary cards, and LOVE LETTERS YOU MIGHT HAVE SAVED.

- Decisions, decisions! What to do with your beautiful, HEIRLOOMED WEDDING GOWN? If you are a widow with children, you might want to keep it for a daughter to wear. If you are divorced, you might prefer to pass it on to someone else who would appreciate it. You might find a bridal rental or resale shop that would buy it.

- Your ENGAGEMENT AND WEDDING RINGS: You can save them for a daughter or daughter-in-law, reset the stones in another piece of jewelry or dispose of the set.

- Check your LINENS. Were you clever enough to choose a man with the same initials? If not, the monogrammed hems on good sheets and pillowcases can be replaced with eyelet lace or embroidered or patterned fabric. Sort through everything and decide which items to keep.

- Your desk will reveal DISPOSABLE ITEMS, such as calling cards, informals and monogrammed letter paper.

- If INITIALS ARE ENGRAVED on your silver, definitely continue to use it. Silver is often passed down from one generation to another, regardless of the initials.

- This is a good time to clear your wardrobe of unwearables, to bring up to date what you can wear and to list items you need to ROUND OUT YOUR TROUSSEAU. Add a smart blouse or sweater to a good skirt; buy new pants to go with that handsome silk shirt. Voila! Two new outfits from one skirt and one shirt! You will remember to shop for lovely new lingerie, of course.

Consider this housecleaning not as a chore but as a joyful preparation for your newfound happiness.

The Nontraditional
Wedding

During the seventies a number of brides preferred to plan unconventional weddings, independent of tradition.

In the eighties the trend reversed, and by the nineties tradition was reestablished, stronger than ever. Today most brides once again want a church wedding dressed in a gown "like their mother wore." A few practices from the nontraditional era remain, however, such as writing one's own vows (if permitted by the clergyman) and adding more personal and individual touches.

Most of this book is directed to those conventional, established customs; this chapter has been written, however, to help the brides who have a sincere desire to carry out their own original and personal ideas in a beautiful way. Because you want your wedding to express your own ideas, all the more reason to make it perfect.

Even the most apparently informal affair cannot happen by itself. For any style of festivity or ceremony, you must decide exactly what you want, then carry it out step by step, carefully, completely and consistently. These three words say it all—*care, completeness* and *consistency.*

As the opening chapter says, not every item will apply to every wedding. Many of the preceding details and reminders, however, need to be considered whether the wedding is to take place in a church or a barn, in a garden or on a hilltop, on the shore or under the sea.

So read all that has gone before and use whatever applies to your plans; next, note the few extra and special reminders for unconventional situations.

SELECTING A LOCATION

If your special dream setting is a mountain peak, a forest, a meadow, a sea- or lakeshore—any isolated out-of-doors location—you need to think of these things:

- A reasonably accessible site.

- Adequate off-the-road parking.

- An alternate roofed location nearby in case of rain, and a few umbrellas in the trunk of the car.

- Accessible shade.

- Privacy—a location least likely to be interrupted by the sounds of picnickers or hikers during the ceremony. Could you be lucky enough to know the

owner of private waterfront or wooded property
who might let you use it for the occasion?

- If you choose a public park, check to see if you can
and should reserve it.

- Will your Great-Aunt Marian be able to manipulate
the terrain with her walker or cane?

- Caution: Sounds do not carry well out of doors.
Plan to speak distinctly during the ceremony; perhaps consider procuring amplification.

WHO WILL OFFICIATE?

Keep in mind that you and your husband-to-be will
marry each other, and that a minister, rabbi, priest,
judge or other official will simply *officiate* at your marriage.

You will find that individual clergymen, even within
the same denomination, often vary in their attitudes toward self-written vows and other changes in ritual.
Because of these differing attitudes, you need to consult early with the officiator of your choice.

- Discuss with utmost frankness your desires, plans
and innovations.

- Find out if he will agree to special demands upon
him. (Need he fly in a plane, mount a horse, sail in
a boat?)

- Discuss how much additional time he will need to perform the ceremony away from his church.

- If you wish two clergymen, each of a different faith, to officiate jointly, consult with each one to complete the necessary arrangements.

- Discuss props. Will he want a raised platform as a focal point for the ceremony? Does he think you will want kneeling cushions?

HOW TO INVITE

When you shop for invitations, you will find an almost limitless and overwhelming number of choices of color, size, design and wording. The variety gives you the opportunity to express your individuality or carry out a theme. Calligraphy is often used effectively for the invitations and addressing. Here are a few additions you should consider:

- Explicit directions and a map if you have chosen a hard-to-find location.

- If outdoors, directions for where to meet in case of rain.

- A joint invitation from the bride and groom's parents?

- Clothing restrictions, i.e., flat shoes, hats.

TRANSPORTATION

The bride's responsibility to arrange transportation for the bridal party to and from the wedding site becomes even more urgent if the location is hard to find. Include the groom's parents in your arrangements, especially if they are from out of town. Be sure to furnish each driver with a map or explicit directions—with a notation of the estimated time needed to reach the destination.

WHAT TO WEAR

What is the picture you wish to create? Is it pastoral? Medieval? Victorian? Casual? If you dress to complete that picture, all will be perfect. Here are some pointers:

- Rich, bright tones are a throwback to the Middle Ages, when brides wore brightly colored gowns trimmed with braid or jewels for their summer outdoor weddings.

- A satin cathedral train among the thistles? Inconsistent, wouldn't you say?

- Your headdress should harmonize with your dress and the setting. You may choose no head covering at all. Here are a few ideas:

  * If out of doors, a short, fluffy, soft veil is pretty.

* A picture hat.

* Harmonizing "costume" headdress.

* Flowers or leaves—using varieties that will not wilt quickly.

* Ribbons or feathers entwined in your hair.

No matter which, your hairdo should be consistent with your outfit, not a showpiece in itself.

♦ Bare feet? Yes, if they add to the total look. No, if it might appear that you forgot your shoes.

♦ Talk over with your husband-to-be what he and the other men will wear and agree on the overall consistent look you want to present. As you know, dinner jackets are never acceptable in the daytime.

FLOWERS AND DECORATIONS

Continue with your own ideas about the look of the wedding, the total effect. Here are a few thoughts:

♦ PREFERABLE TO HOTHOUSE BLOOMS for an outdoor wedding are:

* Varieties of garden flowers.

* Baskets of field flowers if you can use them before they wilt.

* * A single flower.

* * Sheaves of golden wheat. These can add a rich note; be forewarned that in Elizabethan times they signified fertility!

◆ In a natural setting you will usually need little or no DECORATION except for the buffet table.

◆ If you need to transport flowers some distance, be sure to select LONG-LASTING VARIETIES. It is important to harden flower stems to make them last longer. *(See page 52.)* Transport them in tip-proof containers filled with cold water.

WHAT TO SERVE AT YOUR RECEPTION

Although this subject has been fully discussed in the preceding pages, a few additional ideas for special cases follow:

◆ Unless the site of the ceremony is also ideal for your reception, plan to serve REFRESHMENTS ELSEWHERE—your home, a friend's home, rented or public quarters.

◆ If you are engaging a caterer, be certain he can provide PORTABLE REFRIGERATION EQUIPMENT. If you are arranging the reception yourself, obtain coolers for the wine, other beverages and food—even inexpensive Styrofoam containers.

- As for the menu, plan to have FINGER FOOD for ease in serving. If food must go unrefrigerated for any length of time, avoid mayonnaise, cream sauces and custard fillings.

- If your cake is to be in the sun for a while, be sure it has frosting that will keep well. TAKE NO CHANCES that any of your food might spoil.

- Keep in mind that, if you are far from home, there will be no nearby kitchen for your last-minute needs such as a knife or bottle opener. Now is the time to think, plan and check previous chapters and lists so you can PACK EVERYTHING IN ADVANCE. Among other things, you may need folding tables and chairs, cushions or a plastic tarpaulin, and easy-to-pack plastic wineglasses.

MUSIC

Music helps to create and complete the mood you want—pastoral or solemn or festive. Choose your favorite instruments and selections. Consider the following questions and suggestions:

- Among the easily portable instruments are guitars, violins and flutes.

- A small organ can be transported with a little more expense and trouble, as can a harp.

- If you want your guests to join in the singing or responsive reading, arrange to have copies of the "script" distributed.

+ Do you want background music, dance music or both?

+ Consider portable tape or CD players.

+ Don't hesitate to accept the offer of talented musical friends if they want to take part in your wedding festivities as instrumentalists or singers. You can send them a thank-you gift and a photo or two of themselves taken at the wedding.

PHOTOGRAPHS

If you neglect having photographs taken on your special day, you will always regret it. A competent friend may be able to cover your wedding. Even if he is donating his services, talk over the not-to-be-missed pictures with him. Provide him with plenty of film, and after the wedding send him a gift as a thank-you for a difficult job well done.

You can also provide your guests with throwaway cameras so they may snap away at the reception. Before they leave, the guests should return the cameras to you for developing. You might want to send some of these snapshots to your guests in your next holiday greeting card.

OTHER THOUGHTS

- Ecology-minded brides have been known to furnish their guests with birdseed in place of the traditional rice or rose petals—a combination self-clean product and bird feeder.

- If you are far from civilization, be sure to bring a first-aid kit.

A Final Thought

By following all the lists, suggestions and admonitions in this book, you know you have achieved **Your PERFECT Wedding**.

"PERFECT"

- Complete
- Flawless
- Appropriate
- Right
- Impeccable
- Comprehensive
- Excellent

Happy Life!

Barbara Lee Follett

Loulie Hyde Sutro

Important Contacts

You will refer to this vital section often. Note all pertinent information such as names, addresses including e-mail, telephone numbers including cell phones and faxes.

DATE AND TIME OF WEDDING _____

CEREMONY VENUE _____

_____

_____

TIME OF RECEPTION _____

RECEPTION VENUE _____

_____

_____

BRIDAL CONSULTANT _____

_____

_____

OFFICIATOR (CLERGYMAN)_____

_____

_____

CATERER _____

_____

_____

FLORIST _____

_____

_____

PHOTOGRAPHER_____

_____

_____

VIDEO_____

_____

_____

CEREMONY MUSIC_____

_____

_____

RECEPTION MUSIC_____

_____

_____

CAKE SUPPLIER _____

_____

WEDDING DRESS _____

_____

_____

ATTENDANTS' DRESSES _____

_____

_____

USHERS' OUTFITS _____

_____

_____

LIMOUSINES/DRIVERS/TRANSPORTATION _____

_____

_____

VALET PARKING _____

_____

_____

INVITATIONS/STATIONERY _____

_____

_____

OTHER _____

_____

_____

_____

_____

_____

_____

_____

_____

_____

_____

_____

_____

_____

_____

WEDDING PARTY

Parents of the Bride _____

_____

_____

_____

Parents of the Groom _____

_____

_____

_____

Matron of Honor _____

_____

_____

_____

Maid of Honor _____

_____

_____

_____

Best Man _____

_____

_____

_____

Head Usher _____

_____

_____

_____

Usher _____

_____

_____

_____

Usher _____

_____

_____

_____

_____

Usher _____

_____

_____

_____

Usher _____

_____

_____

_____

Bridesmaid _____

_____

_____

_____

Bridesmaid _____

_____

_____

_____

Bridesmaid _____

_____

_____

_____

Bridesmaid _____

_____

_____

_____

Junior Bridesmaid _____

_____

_____

_____

Flower Girl _____

_____

_____

_____

Ring Bearer _____

_____

_____

_____

Guest Book Attendant _____

_____

_____

_____

Other _____

_____

_____
_____
_____
_____
_____
_____
_____

BRIDAL REGISTRY

This is the section to record information including: stores, department personnel and patterns.

_____
_____
_____
_____
_____
_____
_____
_____
_____

NOTES

Index

The late Barbara Lee Follett wrote the first *Check List for a Perfect Wedding* following the marriage of her daughter in the 1950s, drawing on reader comments for the next four editions. Editing the new version with Follett's children, Loulie Hyde Sutro is a writer, family friend, and recent mother-of-two-brides. She lives in Marin County, California.